A GILLNET'S
DRIFT

A GILLNET'S
DRIFT

TALES OF FISH AND FREEDOM
ON THE BC COAST

W.N. MARACH

VICTORIA · VANCOUVER · CALGARY

Heritage House Publishing Company Ltd
heritagehouse.ca

LIBRARY AND ARCHIVES CANADA CATALOGUING IN PUBLICATION

Marach, W. N., author
    A gillnet's drift: tales of fish and freedom on the BC coast / W.N. Marach.

Issued in print and electronic formats.
ISBN 978-1-927527-71-9 (pbk.).— ISBN 978-1-927527-72-6 (html).— ISBN 978-1-927527-73-3 (pdf)

    1. Marach, W. N. 2. Fishers—British Columbia—Pacific Coast—Biography. 3. Gillnetting—British Columbia—Pacific Coast—Anecdotes. 4. Pacific salmon fishing—British Columbia—Pacific Coast—Anecdotes. 5. Pacific Coast (B.C.)—Biography—Anecdotes. 6. Pacific Coast (B.C.)—Description and travel—Anecdote. I. Title.

SH20.M34A3 2014   639.2092   C2013-908556-4 C2013-908557-2

Edited by Kate Scallion
Proofread by Leslie Cameron
Cover and book design by Jacqui Thomas
Cover photos by piola666/iStockphoto.com (front) and wave pattern by
    kimikodate/iStockphoto.com (back)
Frontispiece photo: "Nick Marach mending his nets in Johnstone Strait." Courtesy of the author.
Chapter opener image: StillFX/iStockphoto.com

MIX
Paper from responsible sources
FSC
www.fsc.org   FSC® C016245

The interior of this book was produced on 100% post-consumer recycled paper, processed chlorine free and printed with vegetable-based inks.

Heritage House acknowledges the financial support for its publishing program from the Government of Canada through the Canada Book Fund (CBF), Canada Council for the Arts, and the Province of British Columbia through the British Columbia Arts Council and the Book Publishing Tax Credit.

Canadian Patrimoine
Heritage   canadien

The Canada Council | Le Conseil des Arts
for the Arts | du Canada

BRITISH COLUMBIA
ARTS COUNCIL

18 17 16 15 14 1 2 3 4 5

Printed in Canada

For Catherine, Natalie,
Nicholas, Alexis, and especially Veronica.

| | | | |

Thanks to Rod Bonikowsky and Blaine Parry for
their help in getting me started fishing and for reviewing
the manuscript, and to Archie Neem, Jim Maynes,
and Joe Carr for the memories.

‖‖ CONTENTS ‖‖

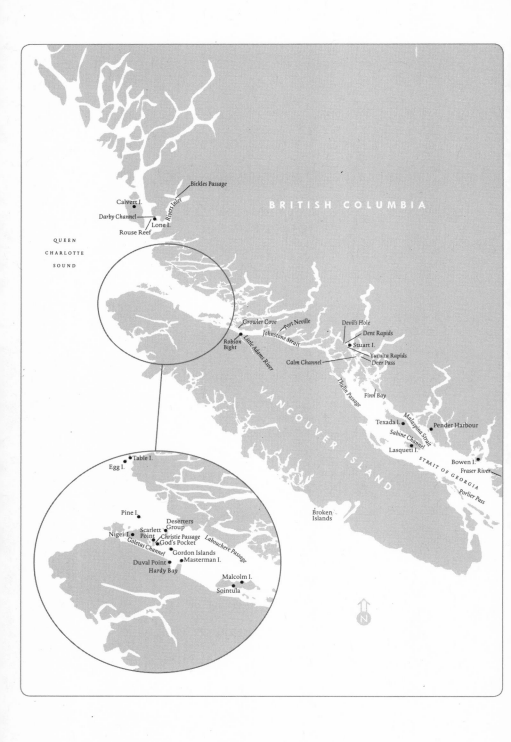

BICKLES PASSAGE

Calvert I.

Darby Channel

Lone I.

Rouse Reef

Rivers Inlet

QUEEN
CHARLOTTE
SOUND

BRITISH COLUMBIA

Growler Cove

Port Neville

Johnstone Strait

Robson
Bight

Little Adams River

Devil's Hole

Dent Rapids

Stuart I.

Yuculta Rapids

Calm Channel

Deer Pass

Thulin Passage

Finh Bay

Texada I.

Malaspina Strait

Pender Harbour

Sabine Channel

Lasqueti I.

Bowen I.

STRAIT OF GEORGIA

Fraser River

Porlier Pass

VANCOUVER ISLAND

Broken
Islands

Table I.

Egg I.

Pine I.

Deserters
Group

Scarlett
Point

Nigei I.

Christie Passage

God's Pocket

Labouchere Passage

Goletas Channel

Gordon Islands

Duval Point

Masterman I.

Hardy Bay

Malcolm I.

Sointula

N

⫴ FOREWORD ⫴

One of the most surprising things about gillnetting forty years ago was how easy it was to get into. The salmon runs were still strong. There were lots of good boats for sale cheap as owners upgraded old wooden boats to new fibreglass ones. Many of the boats being sold were gillnetters from the 1920s and '30s. They were narrow-gutted double-enders with nice lines that slid across the water, leaving no more wake than a duck. A few of them still had two-cylinder Easthope engines, which made a leisurely chuffing sound that was deceptively out of proportion to the speed they were going. If there was ever a symbol of self-expression and freedom, it was going fishing in one of those boats. You didn't have to be a hippie to find that irresistible.

All it took to call yourself a gillnetter was a boat, a net, and a licence. You had acquired a vocation, or more correctly, a status. The benefits of your status kicked in even before you had a net to put in the water. You could buy a whole range of things: fishing equipment, groceries, tools, work clothes, and even mattresses at wholesale prices using your fishing licence. There were special prices for you at the fuel docks and writeoffs on your income tax. You qualified for cheap berth rates at the False Creek Fishermen's Terminal right in the centre of Vancouver. Best of all, you got to be addressed as "skipper" by fisheries officers, even though you might never have been out on a boat before getting your licence. And then, when the season opened, the entire coast of British Columbia became your workplace. There wasn't a vocation in the world that came close to that freedom.

1

||| THE HASTY PURCHASE |||

One Friday morning in the spring of 1972, an ad appeared in the *Vancouver Sun* offering a gillnetter for sale. It caught my eye, not because I wanted to go fishing, but because I was looking for a boat to live on, and the price was cheap.

I was just back in Vancouver after three years away. The first half of that time I'd been working in Toronto, and the second half I'd spent travelling. A recently graduated architect, I'd gone to find some meaning in my profession after the letdown of working in the real world. I didn't have an itinerary or a schedule for my search, but I did have a 1952 BSA motorcycle, bought on impulse in a village near Bath, England, where I had gone to see the ancient Roman ruins. I'd learned to ride it in the street in front of the seller's house, and had ridden it through Europe and part of North Africa before selling it in Rome. Each day brought new adventures, but no enlightenment or the meaning I'd gone looking for. What I did decide—maybe from seeing the converted barges along the Thames embankment or as a reaction to dry camping on the edges of the Tunisian Sahara or merely from experiencing the total freedom of the road—was to live on the water when I got back to Vancouver.

Within a week of getting back, I landed a job with one of the better architectural firms in Vancouver. Their office was in an old house, supposedly a former brothel, on Fairview Slopes. The staff lounge was on the top floor with spectacular views over False Creek and downtown. Although starting time was nine o'clock, a few of us came in early to have coffee in the lounge and read the morning papers before getting down to work.

As was already our routine, my friend Blake had made the first pot of coffee. I poured cups for both of us and pointed out the ad to him. I didn't know anything about gillnetters, and was going on price only. For once, it was in a range I could afford. Blake was the resident expert on things the average architect didn't know much about, fishboats being one of those things. His knowledge of boats was from his boyhood when he'd fished with an uncle who was a gillnetter on the Fraser River.

"Have a look. If you like it, offer him half of what he's asking," he said.

"Looks like it's already about half the price of other gillnetters I've seen in here," I told him.

"Doesn't matter—offer half. You can always come up."

"I don't want to insult the guy."

"Are you kidding? It's only their wives and girlfriends you can insult fishermen about, not stuff like that. Besides, maybe there's something wrong with it," he said.

I called the owner during my lunch break. He said the boat was up on the dry in the BC Packers yard in Steveston, and its name was the *T.K.* The name was a little disappointing, and I was surprised to hear him say "its" instead of "her" when referring to the boat. I'd always thought that any vessel larger that a rowboat was referred to in the feminine. It was my first subtle clue that gillnetters were a little different.

Still on my lunch break, I went to the bank for money. I asked the teller for as many hundred-dollar bills as she had to make my offer more impressive. My father used to say having cash on hand always gave you the advantage in a deal. Remembering Blake's advice, I separated the money into two halves. My plan was to start by offering less than half the asking price and work up from there if I had to. If the boat looked to be a fantastic deal at the asking price, I could always go into the other half of the money, stashed in the inside pocket of my jacket, to improve my offer. If the owner wouldn't accept, or if there was something wrong with it as Blake had suggested, I'd keep looking.

The withdrawal nearly cleaned out my account. I left the bank wondering if I was doing the right thing.

Leaving work right at quitting time, I drove out to the boat yard where the owner had said the *T.K.* was stored. There were plenty of spaces in the parking lot at that time of the day. I got out and went through the gate into a yard that looked to be about an acre in size. From the few boats still braced up on timbers, I gathered that there had been rows of them stored for the winter and then re-floated for the fishing season. The *T.K.* wasn't among the vessels on these timbers. In the far corner of the yard there were another ten boats blocked up in a row. The *T.K.* was among those.

As I got closer, I was surprised at how big the boats seemed, braced up on the timbers. The bows stood nearly twice my height, and their sterns, most with some sort of rollers on them, nearly as high. All of them were wooden boats, some with the planks showing quite clearly through their paint. Nailheads and even plank ends had popped out in several of the hulls. The hull on the *T.K.* was smooth and clean by comparison. It looked freshly painted. Two of the boats had square sterns while the others were pointed at both ends. From what I remembered of Blake's lecture on fishboats, these were called double-enders. Gillnetters preferred double-enders, he explained, because they wouldn't pull nets out of shape in a running tide as quickly as boats with square sterns would. Looking at the two different types of hulls, I thought I could see what he meant. That was the *T.K.*'s first good point, although it shouldn't have mattered since all I was looking for was a live-aboard.

Lying on the ground between the boats was an old, paint-spattered, wooden ladder. I stood it against the side of the *T.K.* and climbed up to have a closer look. The front part of the boat had a low cabin rising out of the deck and a small wheelhouse. The cabin had round portholes on the sides and a small hatch fitted with a skylight. The wheelhouse had windows along the sides and front. Both the cabin and wheelhouse had nicely arched roofs with walls that were rounded in front and curved along the sides to follow the sheer line of the hull. Roof edges were trimmed with a bull-nosed hardwood cap, forming a curve in both vertical and horizontal planes that seduced the eye. The boat was white with dark green decks and trim. The layers of paint slapped on over the years couldn't hide the builder's flawless joinery. It brought back memories of my father in his carpentry shop with wood shavings on the floor as he made things like chairs and fret saws by shaping wood into difficult curves, which showed the joy he took in doing so.

The back part of the boat was obviously the business end. On the deck behind the wheelhouse, there was a canvas-covered hatch over what I assumed was a fish hold. On a solid-looking timber frame beyond that was a large wooden reel. According to Blake's lecture, that was called a drum and it held the net. Bolted to the frame alongside the drum was a large cast iron device that drove it. This was called a drum drive, Blake had said, and the best were Easthopes. I looked closely; there was the Easthope name cast into the side of the drive: yet another point to the good for the *T.K.* It was dawning on me that although all I was looking for was a live-aboard, if the boat came with all the parts needed to go gillnetting, it was an option I might consider—if I ended up the new owner.

There was a payphone at the gate to the storage yard, so I called the owner of the boat. He was showing me through it a half hour later. It was cramped, and I had to stoop in the forward cabin, but everything I needed was there: stove, bunk, storage lockers—again with the nice joinery—and a four-cylinder Gray Marine engine, painted candy-apple red. When I asked about the head, the owner said it was to gillnetter standards: a galvanized bucket with a short piece of rope attached to the handle. It spent the winter upended on the engine exhaust, keeping the rainwater out. He took it down so I could try the engine.

A few cranks of the starter had it running. It was surprisingly smooth for an engine that hadn't run for a while. We shut it down quickly to avoid overheating since the engine coolant ran through a keel cooler that needed to be underwater to work. The sound of that engine had me pretty much sold. All there was left to know was why he was selling the boat. The answer was plausible: he had become a fireman. It was what he'd always wanted to do, even more than fishing. Unfortunately, becoming a firefighter didn't leave him enough time to fish. As much as he regretted it, the boat had to go.

My father used to say "never make an important decision without sleeping on it." Normally, I would have done so, but here was an owner who had just accepted my offer of less than half his asking price. I didn't have to dicker and he seemed relieved it was over. From what I could see, he was one of those people who just was not good at selling things. It was dusk when we shook hands on the deal. I handed over the cash and he gave me the keys.

Neither of us had any paper, so we wrote up a bill of sale on the back of a newspaper flyer I'd found in my car. The wording said the boat was "as is," which I didn't object to since I'd gone over it closely and heard the engine running. Besides, I had confidence in my grasp of such things. There was another document from the Department of Fisheries, something to do with transferring a licence. We both signed the bill of sale and the fisheries document. The fireman suggested I keep them in case they were needed at the fisheries office. I threw them in the glove compartment of my car, on the off chance they would be.

The fireman drove off with his money and I stopped at the payphone at the yard gate, hoping Blake would be home. He was, so I told him about my purchase.

"Sounds good," he said. "Where is it tied up?"

"Uh, it's not in the water yet. It's up on blocks in the BC Packers yard in Steveston."

"Oh, I see."

"But I looked at the hull real close," I told him. "It looked nice and tight, not like some of the other boats there . . ."

"Well, some of them aren't likely to fish again. How long was your boat up on the dry anyway?" I felt myself getting smaller as he asked this.

"Oh man, I dunno; never asked him."

"Ah, he probably would have lied anyway. New paint on it?"

"Looks like it. Doesn't sound good, huh?"

"Well, you never know," he said. "Why don't you try some of the seams tomorrow—a screwdriver or even a quarter will do. If it goes in easy, it ain't ready for the water quite yet. You might need to do some re-caulking, if the plank edges aren't too soft, that is."

"Re-caulking?" I said.

"Yeah, but I've seen it done a few times; it's not that hard. You'll pick it up in no time," he said encouragingly.

"Son of a bitch."

"Yeah, well, you never know, maybe the seams are still good and tight. Re-floating boats after they've been out on the dry for a while is always tricky. One way or the other, they'll all try to fool you."

"Goddamn, son of a bitch," I said.

It was already dark, and I was starving. I might have gone back to try the seams with a quarter right then, but I'd had enough bad news for one night. Instead, I drove back to Vancouver, and found a parking spot on Granville Street close to Love's Skillet Cafe. I went in and ordered a native sirloin, rare. When it came, I was still so angry with myself I had to fight the urge to grab it with both hands and tear the meat off the bone with my teeth. Afterwards, I walked along with the crowds on Granville Street, looking at the marquee lights of the theatres and inhaling the Friday-night smells of pizza and fried onions in the air. That usually made me feel better, but not this time.

Finally I went back to the house where I had rented a room until I could find a boat to live on. No one was up and I went straight to bed, tossing about and cursing myself for being so stupid as to throw most of the money I had in the world into that damn boat. I could just hear what everyone at work would say when Blake told them about my purchase.

The next morning I was at the boatyard soon after daylight. There were already cars parked at the gate and people moving around inside the yard. I parked my car near the others and took a screwdriver out of the toolbox in the trunk in case the quarter didn't work. Walking through the gates, I could see the *T.K.* and its decrepit mates in the distance, as if in quarantine. I hadn't noticed this the previous day for some reason, but seeing them there drove out any hope I had that the seams were tight. Standing in the doorway of what looked like a large workshop, two men were talking as I went by. They might have been gillnetters or biker gang members or both as far as I could tell by their appearance. If they had given me so much as a look, I would have decked them both, or at least gone down trying—such was the effect of that damned boat on my normally sunny disposition.

The walk across the yard to the *T.K.* felt like climbing a moderate hill. Now that I knew what I was looking for, I could see the seams through the paint. Taking a quarter out of my jeans, I tried it on one of them. It slipped in with hardly any resistance. The same thing happened on the next one, and the one after that. Trying the screwdriver gave the same result. Pulling its blade along the seam, I raked out more than a foot of disgusting black material stuck to flaking white paint with no effort at all. Although I had been preparing myself for the worst, this was beyond anything I had imagined.

With the *T.K.* absorbing my curses serenely and unfazed by threats of firebombing, all I had left to consider were Blake's words about re-caulking if the plank edges weren't too soft. Using the screwdriver, I raked out more seams and found that the plank edges seemed fine. Maybe re-caulking was possible. More to the point, it had to be. All I'd need to do was learn how. The more I thought about it, the more possible it seemed.

My father had been a carpenter and cabinetmaker who coaxed magic out of wood with his hands. I was nowhere near as good, but I could handle tools and had even built a speedboat with him when I was a teenager. My carpenter's tools were still in the family home in Ontario, but it didn't seem as if re-caulking a boat needed anything fancy. It stood to reason that the tools and materials I'd need would be stocked in any of the marine supply stores just up the street from the boatyard. Feeling a little more in control of my prospects, I went shopping.

In the window of the first store I came to was a sour-looking grey-haired man peering out into the street. There was no one else in the store, but he didn't seem pleased to see me come through the door. I asked him whether he carried any tools for caulking boats. Without answering, he turned and led me to the back of the store where the shelves held tools and gadgets I'd never seen before. He pulled out a tool that looked like a wide, thick cold chisel with a thin shank, and asked if that was what I had in mind.

"Damned if I know. Is that what they use to pound in the caulking?"

"Yep, depending on what kind of boat," he said. "What kind you got?"

"A double-ender, an old gillnetter."

"Oh-ho, so you got stuck with one of those old ones in the BC Packers yard?" He said it as if I'd just answered a question he'd asked himself when I came in.

"I guess so. There's about ten of them in a row there."

"So that's all there's left there now, huh? Used to be more, but the hippies been buying them up. Most of them sunk now." The way he said it made me think he knew about the problems they'd run into with those old boats, and had somehow taken enjoyment from them.

"I don't know about that. I'm just looking for a live-aboard," I told him.

"You want to live aboard one of those old tubs?" he asked, his eyebrows shooting up a half inch above the top of his glasses. His enjoyment was growing. "Why don't you find a nice apartment instead? Much easier for you, I bet."

"I know, I know. I'm probably nuts, but I like the water, and I'd like to give it a try," I replied. "If you don't mind."

"Oh, I don't mind; I don't mind." He was grinning broadly. "More business for me."

I didn't say anything. His tone was enough to make any business between us impossible. The surprising thing was that he didn't seem to realize it: he kept pulling items needed for caulking a boat off shelves and tossing them onto the counter as if I'd buy them. When he was done he turned toward me, still half-smiling.

"Okay, that's all you need," he said.

I took a close look at what he'd brought out, while he stood by, rocking back and forth slightly and humming to himself.

"All right?" he smirked.

"Nope. It isn't more business for you," I said, and walked out.

I headed for the other marine stores along the street, undecided as to whether I'd won some sort of minor victory for the hippies or proved myself an idiot. Whatever it was, I now knew what I needed to re-caulk the boat, what it looked like, and what it cost—at least in that store. It didn't seem all that complicated. Maybe I could pull it off after all.

There was a café a half block up the street with a good smell coming through the screen door. Taking a window booth, I ordered an early lunch and took stock of my situation. Buying the boat up on the dry had been inexcusably stupid; there was nothing I could do to change that. At least I hadn't tried to launch it with the seams in the condition they were in or I'd have been in far bigger trouble. This way, I could arrange with the fishing company that owned the boatyard to take my time re-caulking the *T.K.* right where it was blocked up on timbers. That would allow me to do the work at my own speed. The good part was that the rest of the boat seemed well built and still sound, and the engine ran well.

It was barely noon when I finished lunch. More people had come in while I was eating, and the little café was buzzing with conversations. I dawdled over my coffee, half-listening to the talk and looking out at the people going by on the sidewalk. They would never have been mistaken for the weekday office crowd in downtown Vancouver. Men far outnumbered the women for one thing, and no one was in a hurry. The sidewalks were busy, but not crowded by downtown standards. There was not a necktie among the men, nor high heels among the women. Instead of suits, there were doeskin shirts, jeans, and fishermen's romeos. Through the back door of the café, I could see rows of gillnet boats on the glinting water of the Fraser River. I guessed the people I was listening to and watching on the sidewalk were from those boats and instinctively liked the look of them. The waitress, who looked like a local high school girl, had brought my bill and poured me another cup of coffee. Ten minutes later she was back with the coffee pot, telling me there was no rush and looking like she meant it, but I had things to do.

By three o'clock I had been to the other marine stores on the street and still hadn't bought a thing. The next day was Sunday and the stores would be closed. If I wanted to get something done that weekend, I needed to make some purchases that afternoon. While deciding where to take my business, I remembered a wholesale marine supply store near the Vancouver waterfront that I'd been in years ago. Taking a chance that it was still open, I headed that way.

Traffic had picked up from the morning and it was nearly four by the time I reached its parking lot and found a space for my car. The store was much larger than the ones in Steveston, and I lost track of time as I wandered the aisles. It was a busy place, with customers two deep along the front of the sales counters and clerks scurrying about behind them. The activity, I finally realized, was because it was nearly closing time. If I was going to be served before the store closed, I had to get into the line up at the front counter. I found a place behind a couple of shorter customers at the counter, thinking that if I used my height, I could easily catch the eye of the first clerk who became free.

It worked; a clerk, an older man with the collar buttoned to the top of his flannel shirt, looked at me, then at the clock, and back at me again.

"What are you after, son?" he asked in a kindly way.

I told him, and he came out from behind the counter and led me down one of the aisles. By now the crowd in the store was thinning and one of the clerks was standing beside the door, which was locked, and letting people out.

What I wanted was in an area at the end of an aisle. The clerk got an empty box from under a display case and slid it along the floor to where we were going. He wasn't in a hurry, even though now it was a few minutes to closing time and there weren't many customers left in the store. I noticed that there was only one other clerk left behind the sales counters.

"So you're going to re-caulk your boat, are you?" he asked with the precise diction of a CBC announcer.

"Yeah, I am. Never did it before, but I'm going to give it a good try."

"That's the spirit," he said with a smile. "I've heard it's not all that hard once you get the knack."

As we talked, he picked the items I needed off the shelves and held them up for my approval before putting them into the box.

"Looks like that should do it," I said, remembering everything that the clerk in Steveston had shown me.

"Righty ho," he said. "Sounds like you know what you're doing. What about caulking cotton? How much do you think you'll need?"

So much for knowing what I was doing. "Er, I dunno. It's a thirty-two-foot boat; does that help?"

"It does," he said, and appeared to do a quick calculation in his head. "You might start with a dozen then. That will likely be too many, but what you don't use, you can bring back. There's nothing worse than running out midway through the job."

He tossed the caulking cotton into the box, and I picked it up and followed him to the sales counter. There were only two of us left in the store by then, although I could hear clerks shouting and laughing through the back wall.

"Sounds like those guys are starting their weekend already," I said.

"Every chance they get," he said. "Got your commercial card?"

"My what?"

"Your commercial card. You are a commercial fisherman, aren't you? You know this is a wholesale business and we can't sell to you unless you are ... "

"Yeah! I am! At least I will be. I just bought the boat." I could feel my face going red.

"You aren't stringing me a line, are you, son? If you are, I'll have to kick you out and you'll never be allowed in here again." He said it in a kindly, patient way that had far more effect than if he'd raged at me.

"No, no, I'd never do that," I said, then remembering the papers in the glove compartment, I almost shouted: "Hey! I've got the sales papers in the car! Can I get them for you?"

"Yes, I think you'd better," he said drily.

He held the door open as I sprinted to the car and back. Taking the papers from me at the door, he looked them over carefully, and then gave me a sharp glance.

"All right. I probably shouldn't, but you look like you could use a break. I'll just copy your commercial plate number on the invoice by hand, like you've lost your card. But make sure you take the transfer papers to fisheries on Monday."

"Oh, man, thanks. Don't worry. I'll be there first thing!"

The clerk's head was down, but he looked like he was smiling to himself as he carefully hand-lettered my invoice. It was a half hour after closing time by then, but he still wasn't in a hurry. He chatted about the pleasures of working on wooden boats while he finished the invoice and entered the items into the cash register. I couldn't see him building boats, or doing anything manual with his small, clean hands. Everything about him looked soft and rounded: cheeks, nose, forehead, shoulders, back, and stomach—even his eyes that looked out timidly from behind rimless glasses. He reminded me of a university professor who lectured on the proper way certain things had to be done on knowledge solely drawn from books without ever having done them himself. Despite that, he was likeable. When he presented me with the invoice, I had a quick look before paying him from the cash I had left over from the deal on the boat. I noticed that the prices were about a third less than the ones in Steveston, and decided that this was the store for me. I also noticed that he had printed "Mac" in the box for the salesman's name. He held the door open as I carried out my box.

"Thanks, Mac," I said. "You've restored my faith in humanity."

He laughed. "Just don't forget where you have to go Monday, or I'll be out of a job."

2

⫴ THE DECKHAND ⫴

It was early evening when I got back to the house. The refrigerator was full of party food and the usual pile of dishes around the sink had been put away. A sign advised against messing up the kitchen. Thus warned, I had a shower, changed, and went out again to have a late dinner, feeling quite satisfied with the way the day had gone. The evening was showing promise too. One of the people invited to the party was a girl I'd heard a lot about and was looking forward to meeting.

By the time I got back to the house, the party had started. It wasn't so much a party as a get-together. There were still parking spots on the street in front of the house, and the music wasn't blasting so much as murmuring. I knew most of the people there and they weren't the type to howl long into the night. It occurred to me, as I found my way to the refrigerator for a beer, that we had all gotten older. It was an odd thought to begin a night that was supposed to be fun.

There were knots of people in the kitchen, dining room, and living room of the house, but there was no sign of the girl I was supposed to meet among them. I moved around, nursing my beer and doing more listening than talking. The evening was quickly becoming a bore. It was partly, I thought, because I hadn't been back in Vancouver long enough to catch up on the things everyone was excited about. Mixed in with the gossip, I caught snippets about new restaurants opening, clothing styles changing, and couples divorcing, none of which would have interested me anyway. I could have chipped into the conversation with the fascinating things I'd seen in Tunisia only two months earlier, or the boat I was fixing to re-caulk, but they didn't seem like the audience for anything like that. After another hour, I decided to give up on the night, get a glass of milk, and go up to my room to read. It had turned into that kind of party.

When I got to the kitchen, a girl was at the refrigerator. She turned to face me. The music was loud enough that she wouldn't have heard me come in, but she must have sensed something. She was dark-haired with the brown eyes and olive skin of some of the Arab women I'd seen in North Africa, and pretty.

"I think I'm supposed to meet you," I said.

"Yes, and me you," she replied.

We found a quiet corner and talked. I told her about my disillusionment with architecture, the utter joy of roaming Europe and Tunisia on a motorcycle, and my stupid purchase of a derelict old fishboat.

"My life is dull by comparison," she said. She was a social worker with the City of Vancouver, getting people off the streets and into shelters. "Some of those old guys are so far gone they don't even know what money is about," she said.

In the evenings she worked on her master's degree in anthropology on Northwest Coast Indian myths. "If I don't pay him enough attention, Fred, my cat, jumps up and stretches out right across my thesis papers," she said. Lucky cat, I thought.

Midnight slipped by, two in the morning, then we noticed we were the last ones at the party. She said she had to get up early the next day and needed to get home. I offered her a ride, but she'd come in her own car. We walked out to it and she put her hand into mine to say goodnight. I took the keys she found after a little rummaging in her purse, opened the car door for her, closed it after she got in, and stood watching her drive off until she was out of sight.

Our first date was a week later. It almost didn't happen. I asked if she would be interested in going to a party at a beach house my firm's senior partner had on Mayne Island. She told me she'd already made plans and didn't think she could change them. When the day came, I was putting a few things in the trunk of my car before leaving for the ferry terminal when I noticed a red Volkswagen Beetle coming down the street at a good clip. It was hers. She pulled up even with me and leaned out the window. My heart leapt.

"I've changed my plans," she said. "I'm coming with you, or have you already made other arrangements?"

"No," I said, trying not to grin like an idiot, "I haven't."

We drove my car to the terminal, parked it, and caught the Mayne Island ferry at the last minute. The party was at a beach-front house a short walk from the ferry terminal. Although she didn't know anyone there, she did better than I at keeping up our end of conversations with people I knew. That might have been because I couldn't keep my attention from wandering back to her. We drifted outside after a while and walked down the beach until the sound of the party became faint. She knelt down and turned over a stone at the water's edge, like a child would, and watched as a tiny crab scuttled away. She did little unsophisticated things like that which were irresistible.

Busy as we were, we found more and more time for each other. By July, it was every evening.

Her name was Valerie. She was sharing a house with four other girls off Alma Street in Point Grey. One day, after we'd known each other for a few months, she said she was thinking of moving out and finding a place of her own. I volunteered to help her search. Each evening we'd check the newspaper for ads under "suites for rent," mark the ones she thought looked interesting, and drive around for a look at the building and its location. We developed a system: I'd drive and she'd fall asleep. Being a passenger in a car tended to make her sleepy, especially in those days with her job, master's degree, and late nights with me.

After a few weeks of searching, we found a suite she liked in a grand old house on Twelfth Avenue across from City Hall. The suite was made up of the original drawing room and an adjoining sunroom on the ground floor. The main room had a tiled fireplace that still worked and a large bay window. The sunroom, which was separated from the main room by French doors, had windows on three sides and had been converted into a kitchen and dining area. After helping her move in, I stayed to watch how she made sure Fred, her cat, would take to the new place and not run away. She did it by putting butter on his paws. It must have worked, because next morning he was still there. So was I.

With the change in my intentions to live on the water, the question became what to do with my intended live-aboard. Even if I had wanted to sell it, the ongoing re-caulking, slowed by my involvement with Valerie, made it unlikely. By then I didn't want to anyway. The idea of using it as the fish-boat it was intended to be had taken hold. Besides, the *T.K.* was licensed for the current year as an A-licensed fishboat. That meant I could use it to fish salmon anywhere on the coast by gillnet or troll gear, but not by both at the same time.

Back when I renewed my licence after buying the caulking gear —a matter of filling out a few forms and spending a couple hundred dollars—I knew I was only kidding myself that the boat was just a live-aboard. I justified it by saying renewing the licence was to keep the *T.K.*'s value up for re-sale and to get a card to buy stuff wholesale, but even then I knew it was only a matter of time before I got a net and went fishing.

When I resumed caulking, my friend Don gave me a hand. I knew him from architecture college, but he was not the typical architecture student, who, in those days, wore turtleneck sweaters and listened to cool jazz. He dressed like Johnny Cash and knew all there was to know about country-and-western music. I first saw him during enrolment week at UBC. He was dressed all in black: boots, jeans, belt, shirt, bolo tie, and hat. Tall and lean, he was standing on the hood of his black 1952 Chevrolet sedan parked in front of the architecture building, haranguing a puzzled crowd of students about voting for the Social Credit Party candidate in the next election. As gaunt and passionate as an old Bolshevik, he was on a liberal university campus shilling for a political party that was as far right as any that had existed in this country. A bundle of contradictions like that was hard to resist. We became friends right off.

The *T.K.* was hoisted back into the water the day after we finished caulking. It was late afternoon when Don and I tied it up near the hoisting dock. He left for home and I went out to the telephone at the yard gate to tell Valerie I was no longer a dry-land skipper. When I got back to the boat, I heard the sound of water. It was more of a gush than a trickle, and seemed to be loudest in the fish hold. Jumping down into it, I lifted the bottom planks and saw water welling up where the propeller shaft went through the keel fitting. Part of the shaft was already submerged. The electric bilge pumps were on, but not making much headway.

I climbed out of the hold and ran up the dock to see if the boat hoist crew was still around. They had already gone, and the boat hoist was parked and locked up. As I ran back to the boat, it seemed to be sitting lower in the water. Jumping back into the fish hold, I landed in water that was now covering the bottom of the hold. On my knees, I plunged my hand into where I had seen the water welling up. The first thing I felt was the large nut on the drive shaft, where it went into the stuffing box. The nut was loosened off and turned easily by hand. As I tightened it onto the fitting, the gush of water slowed. I had looked at the fitting when the boat was out of the water and didn't notice the nut was backed off. Since tightening the nut hadn't completely stopped the leak, I deduced from the fitting's name that it must have contained some sort of stuffing, which had dried out from the boat being out of the water. I had to do something about it very soon.

That night I slept aboard. Despite my dreams of the boat sinking, it was still afloat in the morning, although the bilge pumps were getting a workout. As soon as the marine stores opened, I bought a coil of stuffing. The clerk said the boat had to be out of the water to put it in, but I found a simpler way. The *T.K.* had a small Jabsco pump for washing down the decks. I spliced a section of garden hose to its intake and used it to suction out the water coming in when I backed off the nut and slid it up the shaft. Winding a half dozen turns of stuffing around the shaft, I forced it into the stuffing box by tapping down on the nut until the threads caught and I was able to turn it the rest of the way. The leaking stopped so quickly it was amazing. I called Valerie in triumph, and she said breakfast would be ready when I got home.

My next concern was the engine. Running it while tied up at the dock hadn't shown any problems. The spark plugs looked good, but I installed new ones anyway. The rotor and points looked fine so I left them alone, but I added them to the list of spare parts to buy when I found a dealer that had parts for older model Gray Marine engines. The engine temperature had remained stable, but the water pump worried me. It was driven by a short external shaft that had flimsy-looking rubber connectors. All I could do was hope it would keep working. I made a note of a few spare rubber connectors I found in a box of parts in one of the compartments in the trunk cabin in case of trouble. The engine looked clean enough with no signs of oil leaks at the gaskets, and it continued to run smoothly. I was cautiously confident that it could take us wherever we wanted to go—and bring us back again.

The next step was sea trials. With Don aboard, dressed in black like the first time I'd seen him, right down to the cowboy hat and boots, we set off early one Saturday morning like a marine version of the Deadwood Stagecoach. It was the first time I had driven anything bigger than a sixteen-foot runabout with a thirty-horsepower Johnson outboard, and it was exhilarating. The boat ran perfectly. It seemed fast, responded to the wheel crisply, and was stable cutting through the wake of passing vessels. My confidence grew every minute at the wheel.

The surprise came on our way back to the dock. As we angled in, I threw the engine into reverse to slow down, but there was no response. I had throttled down for the approach, but there was enough momentum to make our meeting with the dock a crash landing. I yelled for Don to hold on. Instead, he timed his leap onto the dock to the last split second and somehow managed to get his shoulder into the bow to reduce the impending collision to a glancing blow. It was a stunt that would have been a credit to Spiderman, let alone a city dude in cowboy boots and a Stetson he managed to keep on his head the whole time.

Once we finally got the *T.K.* roped in and tied up to the dock, I crawled into the engine room to look for the trouble.

After an hour of staring at the drive gear trying to relate its workings to cars, which I knew a little more about, the only thing I could think of was a clutch problem. Getting at it would have meant separating the drive gear from the engine. If it had been a car, I would have dived in with wrenches and hammers, but this was different altogether. I might have tried it anyway, but wary of offending the boat gods in charge of the *T.K.*, I went looking for a mechanic. By then I knew a few people on the docks and was given a contact number for a moonlighter who worked for one of the marine engine dealers. I met him at the boat one evening after work. He knew what the trouble was right away: the boat had not been run for so long that the clutch plates had dried out. The repairs were made that evening, and I paid him from the last of my cash left over from when I bought the *T.K.*

With the *T.K.* finally operable, I took it out for a test drive and promptly found another problem: I wasn't much of a skipper. To correct that, I took practice runs on the river at every chance. Most of my problems came up on docking, especially when a falling tide added to the river current. I should probably have practised a little more before taking Valerie for a ride. The cruise out in the river went smoothly, but coming back to the dock, we hit it with more of a hip-check than a nudge. I jumped out with the bow line in hand to tie up, but forgot that I'd left the engine in reverse. With the boat backing away from the dock, I snubbed the mooring line around a cleat in a desperate attempt to stop it. Fighting the engine and the current while looking nonchalant for Valerie's sake, I finally got it hauled in and tied up. As soon as I got back aboard, I quickly slipped the gear into neutral.

"What was that you did?" Valerie asked.

"Oh, just making sure it was in neutral before shutting down the engine. How did you like the ride? See what I mean about the current in this river?"

"It was fun," she said. "But why did you just move that little lever up?"

The rope burn I got from pulling the boat in was starting to bleed. It saved me from having to answer.

"What's wrong with your hand?" she said, taking it in hers. "Oh, yuck! Where do you keep the bandages?"

"Uh, I don't have any. Besides, it's worse than it looks . . . er." I stammered.

"Oh brother, and you're working with tools that have sharp edges." She rummaged around in her purse and came up with a small pack of tissues. "Do you have any tape to hold this?"

All I had was black electrical tape. She took a strip from the roll by biting a notch with her teeth and tearing the rest with her fingers, as if she'd done it all her life, then wrapped it around my hand to keep the Kleenex in place.

"Keep your hand above your shoulder," she instructed. "It'll help stop the bleeding." I tucked it under my armpit instead, probably just to show her I was still the skipper of my boat.

"Okay, guess where we're going next," she said.

On our way to the drugstore, I fumbled with the lock as we left the boat. She took it from me and snapped it into place. Once we were on the dock she looked over the way I'd left the lines and asked, "Don't you want the stern tied up?"

She wasn't asking; she was telling. I showed her how to tie the mooring line with a clove hitch on the dock's edge timber and she got it on the first try.

"Pretty good, huh?" she said.

"Yep, you know what, now that I think of it . . . " I began.

"Oh, oh, now what?" she asked.

"Well, you know, this is a gillnetter, licensed and all, and the gear is all working. All I need is a net," I began, expecting a short conversation ending in "no."

33

"I think you'd be crazy not to," she said. "You're not exactly using it as a live-aboard now, you know." There was no arguing with her logic.

"Yeah, that makes sense, but that wasn't what I was going to ask you."

"Sure, I'll be your deckhand," she said. "I think it'll be kind of fun."

The weekend after Valerie said she'd be my deckhand, I took the *T.K.* from the dock in Steveston to the False Creek Fishermen's Terminal in Vancouver. Don invited himself along for the ride, claiming there were sandbars in English Bay he could help me avoid because of his superior chart-reading ability and more cautious nature. He came along disguising his cautious nature in the same outfit he'd worn when we took the boat out for its first run. The trip went well until we rounded Point Grey. Don consulted the charts and suggested I steer a course well out into English Bay before turning into False Creek. That was needlessly cautious from what I could see, and I steered a line halfway between his suggestion and my preferred route, which was much closer to shore. Even so, we caught the outer edge of Spanish Banks. Luckily, I had noticed mud being kicked up in our wake, and started to angle farther out into English Bay before we ground to a stop. By working the boat back and forth, and with a lot of luck, I managed to slide it off the bank and into deeper water before the falling tide hung us up on the mud for all of Vancouver to see. After a passage like that, entering the False Creek Fishermen's Terminal for the first time wasn't so much a triumph as a relief.

A few days later, a sign appeared on the bulletin board at the top of the float where the *T.K.* was tied up advertising a gillnet for sale. There was a phone number and an address. The address wasn't far away. The seller was a frail old lady, a gillnetter's widow, who was living with her sister in one of the three-storey walk-ups along Broadway in East Vancouver. The net was in a storage space in the basement of the building. She wanted to get rid of it because there was no room for anything else there, which was unfair to her sister. Both of them took me down to show me what she meant.

There was no elevator. The ladies, with their fluffy slippers, flowery house dresses, and blue-tinted hair, gingerly led me down two flights of stairs to the net. We stood gazing at it wordlessly. It was as alien to that space as a chunk of meteorite. Neatly tied up in the same sort of net cover as those I'd seen on nets stored at False Creek, it felt heavier than all of us combined. It did seem to slide readily enough on the highly polished linoleum floor, though. There was a wide corridor with the same flooring between the storage room and a set of double doors leading outside, which must have been how the net was horsed into the storage room in the first place. I could see myself getting it out the same way. My only problem was that the net was far too big and awkward to fit in the trunk of my car. The widow agreed to a fifty-dollar deposit to keep the net for me while I went to arrange for a truck.

Later that week Valerie sold her red Volkswagen Beetle, which was developing potentially expensive transmission problems. A used blue Datsun pickup truck was bought and the net was its first cargo. That night Valerie and I used the winch at the False Creek Fishermen's Terminal to transfer the net from the truck to the cockpit of the *T.K.*, just as I'd watched the real gillnetters do.

All there was left to do was wait for the next salmon opening in the Strait of Georgia and get that net in the water to do its job. After all I'd been through to get to this point, things could only get better.

3

||| THE ONE-LEGGED GILLNETTER |||

After the move to False Creek, the first person I invited to have a look at the *T.K.* was my friend Blake. I had an ulterior motive: now that I had a net and a boat, I needed someone to teach me gillnetting. None of my other friends even knew the difference between a gillnetter and a seiner, but Blake seemed to remember most of what he'd learned from fishing with his uncle on the Fraser River. I was hoping he would come out for my first attempt at gillnetting. If he didn't, I was sure I could manage, although all I'd have to go on was my instincts. Wherever these instincts came from, it wasn't from any background in commercial fishing. And they weren't from anything I had absorbed fishing the lakes and creeks of my boyhood either. If anything, they were the sort of survival instincts that come from learning how to swim by being thrown off the end of a dock. Whatever it was that kept me from drowning then was what I'd be counting on to see me through my first try at gillnetting.

The office where Blake and I worked wasn't far from the False Creek Fishermen's Terminal. We went down together during our lunch break a couple of days before that week's sockeye opening was announced. His face lit up when he saw the *T.K.* He said it was like the very boat he remembered from fishing with his uncle. Once aboard, he showed me how all the gear worked. He explained how to get the net out of the bundle and onto the drum properly, and how to start making the set. In the years I'd known Blake, I had never seen him so animated. I didn't have to ask; it would be his pleasure, he said, to go out with me on my first night gillnetting.

Two days later we were standing in the cockpit of the *T.K.*, watching the corks of my gillnet dancing in the rippled water. It was early dusk, halfway through the opening, which lasted from eight o'clock that morning until eight o'clock the following morning. We went out after finishing our day's work at the architectural office with kisses from our girl-friends, sandwiches they had made, and thermoses of coffee. If fishing didn't turn out, at least there was enough food for an all-night picnic we joked.

It was mid-August, and much of the gillnet fleet was still up north in Rivers Inlet and other places I'd never seen but was beginning to hear about. The boats that were fishing this opening were spread out thinly over the fishing area. Most of them seemed to be around the Sandheads Light, off the mouth of the Fraser River. We found a spot near the end of the jetty at the North Arm of the Fraser. Blake had shown me how to tie on my shiny new scotchman, the inflatable red buoy used by gillnetters to mark the end of their net, and how to throw it out to begin the set. I took over from there.

Once I had the full length of the net set out, I saw things that were beyond my ability to have imagined. The gill-netters I had gotten to know talked about a net being two hundred fathoms long, which, in units I could relate to, was twelve hundred feet, nearly a quarter mile. It wasn't until I saw my net stretched out behind the boat that I realized how long that actually was. The thought of all the things that could happen to it over that distance was terrifying. Before I had my first sockeye aboard, I learned about tide rips and what they did to a gillnet. One came out of nowhere as we stood in the cockpit admiring the first set of my life. It passed through the net and pulled it into a sharp kink, filling it with kelp, sea grass, tree bark, and a log nearly as long as the boat. Rescuing the net from that mess took a couple of hours. It brought home how little I knew about reading the sea, and proved the terrible vulnerability of a gillnet once it had been set. What grated the most was that in the aftermath, I couldn't remember landing my first sockeye, which had been caught somewhere among the debris.

The log was the worst of the tide rip's leavings. Caught in the last few hundred feet of the net, it was floating so deep in the water I didn't notice it until half the net had been cleaned and brought aboard. Reeling in the net to that point brought the *T.K.*'s stern up to the log's end. Touching it sent a shudder through the boat as if it had hit a reef. The log was black and as broad as a hippo's back. My first efforts to get free of it produced nothing but torn web. It looked buoyant enough to support me, and I thought about climbing out onto it to peel my net off. As I was getting desperate enough to try, the end of the log edged to one side of the *T.K.*'s canoe stern. It continued to scrape along the side of the boat, as if trying to break free on its own. Strands of net slid free, while others popped in bursts like shots fired from tiny Uzis. Efforts with the pike pole to speed it along merely tore up more net, so I left it to make its own way. After a half hour of rumbling and grinding along the side of the boat, the log was gone and I had the net, badly torn, but safe on the drum.

Luckily, the sea had been glass calm throughout that first set. Cleaning the net and getting free of the log had taken so long that it was nearly dark by the time I started to make the next set. Blake had shown me how to attach both the scotchman and a lantern to its end. The lantern was for marking the end of the net in the dark, but since it was a long twilight at that time of the year, the scotchman was needed until it was dark enough for the lantern to be seen. I had made the lantern by copying ones I had seen on the gillnetters tied up near the *T.K.* Simple but effective, it was no more than an ordinary coal oil hurricane lantern fixed to a round plywood plate that was lashed to an inflated car inner tube. Watching it after setting out the net, I was reminded of a duck as it crested wavelets that seemed to be steadily growing in size.

The last of the sunset had left the sky streaked with orange along the western horizon. The water around us had turned dark green. The bluffs of Point Grey were deep purple, and now seemed much closer than they had during the day. Navigation lights had begun blinking for the night. I'd had the sense to buy a chart and study it well enough to recognize the lights off Spanish Banks, the North Arm jetty, Sandheads, and Point Atkinson. The gillnetters around us had their fishing lights on, and brightly lit lanterns danced at the end of their nets. Farther out to sea were the running lights of a freighter angling in toward English Bay. Approaching from the same direction was a jetliner, dropping out of the sky on its way to a landing at the international airport in Richmond. Captivated by all this, I hadn't noticed how quickly the sea was changing.

The light chop I had noticed when watching the lantern had grown into three-foot waves. The boat was rolling and bucking in ways I hadn't seen in the few practice runs I'd taken. The hull creaked and groaned as if getting ready to twist apart. There was another sound too: water surging back and forth in the bilges. Red indicator lamps on the dash lit up as the electric bilge pumps worked with increasing frequency. I watched them, remembering what an old-timer had told me one day back when I was re-caulking the *T.K.*

"That's a cannery boat," he said. "Built by Japs it was. Great boat builders they was. But ya gotta remember them garboards'll leak when it gets lumpy."

"Garboards?" I asked.

"Yeah, the garboards. Planks up against the keel. Seams'll open up," he cackled. "But ya sure won't hafta worry about keepin' them bilges fresh."

He'd wandered off before I could ask him anymore, like what he'd meant by "lumpy," and I'd forgotten about him until I saw the bilge pump lights coming on.

From what I could see of the water being pumped out of the hull fittings, I must have had the freshest bilges in the fleet. What worried me was that the pumps hardly stopped, and the change from a calm sea to what was coming at us now was like nothing I had encountered before. Blake was as close to looking worried as I'd ever seen him.

"Whadaya think?" I asked, shouting to be heard above the noise of the roiling water and protesting boat.

"I dunno," he shouted back, not in his usual laconic manner. "We must be in a flood tide fighting the Fraser outfall. Did you bring a tide table?"

"A what?"

"Never mind," he yelled. "It looks calmer farther out from the river mouth. Maybe you should pick up and re-set out there."

He didn't have to say it twice. I ducked into the wheelhouse to start the engine.

The starter cranked, but it didn't fire on the first try, or the second. A flutter of concern began in my solar plexus. It spread as I tried a third and fourth time without any sign of life from the engine. A few more tries and I resigned myself to crawling down into the heaving darkness of the engine room to look for the trouble. I'd fought with cranky engines in the past, and usually won, but they had been in cars and trucks on solid ground, not in the bottom of an old boat tossing around on dark water. The mere thought of what I had to do was making me seasick.

The engine room was under the wheelhouse, reached through a trapdoor. There was a light down there, but it didn't work. Blake shone the flashlight as I lowered myself down alongside the engine. The first thing I noticed was that bilge water was up over the bottom of the engine and beginning to surge onto the trunk cabin floor. Not only had the engine quit, but the electric bilge pumps weren't keeping up with the leaking garboard seams. My boat was in danger of sinking on our very first night fishing.

The engine looked small and impotent. It was about half as old as the boat itself, likely nearing the end of its life, and any number of things might have gone wrong. Suspecting the trouble was dirt clogging the carburetor, I started by taking the glass reservoir bowl off the bottom of the fuel filter. Finding dirt in it would have been a sign that the carburetor was plugged. By taking the bowl off, I spilled some gasoline. One whiff and my already queasy stomach erupted. Vomit spattered that candy-apple chunk of useless iron. The fumes must have cleared my brain though, because I suddenly thought to check the coil. Squirming around to the other side of the engine to reach it, I saw the problem: the lead wire was dangling loose. I rammed it back into the terminal, made sure it was tight, and clambered back up into the wheelhouse. Holding my breath, I tried the starter again.

This time, after a few tries, the engine caught and purred away as if nothing had happened. I punched the air more in relief than triumph and looked around at Blake. He had a funny look on his face.

"See that tug over there?" he said. "I think it just ran over your net."

"What? What the hell are you talking about? What tug?"

"That tug," he said, holding out his arm like a cop directing traffic. "And you'd better hold on, his wash is going to hit us right quick."

I looked around to where he was pointing. My night vision had been affected by working in the flashlight beam and all I saw was a black shape moving fast toward the North Arm jetty light. The wash was on us a few seconds later. It hit the *T.K.* broadside, heeling the boat over so far I thought we'd capsize. If it weren't for Blake's warning, I might have been thrown overboard.

Blake could utter the longest, most colourful string of profanities of anyone I knew. It was a performance that made people stop what they were doing to listen. He let loose some of his best at the tugboat skipper. For the moment, my elation at starting the engine was forgotten, and the extent of the disaster that had befallen my net wasn't registering. What the tug hadn't affected was the sense that my boat was in danger of sinking. I'd noticed its sluggish recovery after the tugboat's wash had hit, and that the cockpit scuppers were shipping water. The red lights on the dash showing the electric bilge pumps operating were burning steadily now. Even so, the boat seemed to be lower in the water by the minute. The last resort was a manual bilge pump beside the edge of the fish hold. Three inches in diameter, the pump was made of soldered sheet metal that looked like some farmer's creation for filling watering troughs for his animals. It could move water fast. I leapt for it and began to pump like mad.

After half a dozen priming strokes, bilge water began to gush out of the pump's spout in torrents. The water poured out onto the deck so quickly it overloaded the main scuppers, leaving me standing ankle-deep in water. I hadn't had time to change into gumboots after getting out of the engine room. A new pair of running shoes was being ruined, but nothing could have made me happier just then. After each of us took a turn at the pump, the *T.K.* became noticeably more buoyant. I began to think this first night's fishing might be survivable after all. With a new optimism, I started to reel in the net, fervently hoping Blake was wrong about the tug.

He wasn't. The first sign was that the lantern at the end of the net kept drifting away rather than approaching the boat as I hauled the net aboard. Then, with about half of the net in, the cork line started to become gradually stiffer until it felt like wire cable. Blake thought it was from being stretched to extremes just before snapping as the tug had ploughed through the net. A few dozen more fathoms of net came in like that, and then there was no more cork line at all, only a tangle of web twisted around the lead line, emerging slowly from the dark water. Abruptly, even that stopped coming. All I could see of the rest of my net was the lantern tossing in the waves.

Released from the stabilizing effect of the net in the water, the boat edged around until it was crossways to the sea, and went back to its wild rocking. Holding onto the roller brackets, I looked around to get my bearings. A quarter moon fought with a racing cloud cover, throwing a faint wash of light on patches of waves. Although most of the boats were farther to the south, around the mouth of the main arm of the Fraser, one of them was particularly close, and my lantern seemed to be drifting toward it. Leaving the deck pump to Blake, I put the *T.K.* in gear to head that way. As we got closer, I turned on the spotlight and picked up a tangle of corks bunched around my lantern, with the cork line trailing off into the black water. The other boat was less than half a net's length away by then. The skipper had turned on his work light and was picking his net. There seemed to be a fish for every fathom he was bringing in.

Getting the *T.K.* close enough to the mess of corks for Blake to reach with the pike pole took a couple of tries in the pitching sea. Finally he caught hold of the trailing end, pulled it aboard, and tied it to a cleat. I began to tow the end away from the corks around the lantern, hoping to untangle the mess. Somehow it worked, and once the corks were in line, I hand-pulled the remains of the net in. It formed a pathetic little mound on the cockpit deck that I topped with the still burning lantern. To my surprise, we had drifted to within a boat's length of the other gillnetter. He had finished picking his set and was watching us. We were close enough to see that his boat was dirty and unkempt. The skipper was bald and bare-headed with a gaunt face and great Slavic cheekbones. He was wearing what looked like a grey business suit under his apron. He stared at us fiercely.

"How's it going?" I shouted at him, trying to be friendly.

There was no answer or change in the way he was looking at us.

"Did you see the tug that cut my net?" I yelled.

He didn't reply. It was as if I wasn't there.

"Hey, can you hear me?" I tried again.

This time he shouted back, either in gibberish, or some language I couldn't place at all. He gestured at us as if firing pistols, or maybe releasing thunderbolts. He ended his display with a wave of his hand at us in the old European gesture of dismissal and turned his back. He took off his apron and, stuffing it somewhere alongside the drum, began to clamber out of the cockpit toward the wheelhouse. He had to turn toward us to do this. I noticed it *was* a double-breasted suit he was wearing and all the buttons in the jacket were done up. I also noticed he was missing his entire right leg.

Using his hands on grab rails and along the low-set boom much like an ape, he pulled himself along the deck and threw himself into the wheelhouse door. A moment later there was a blast of smoke out of the exhaust as he wheeled his boat around. It looked like he was going to ram us, but at the last moment he cut over and passed across the bow, missing it by inches. His wash put the *T.K.* into another rolling frenzy that had us grabbing for the rigging to keep from being thrown overboard. He roared away, swerving from side to side in what I took to be some form of mock salute to us.

"Whoa, who let him out?" Blake asked after the rocking subsided.

"I guess he didn't like how close we'd drifted to him."

"We weren't that close. More likely he's just plain nuts."

"They aren't going to believe this at the office," I said to Blake as the one-legged man roared off into the dark.

"Never mind the office; I don't believe this, and I was there."

|||||

Later on, when I got to know some of the other gillnetters who tied up at the False Creek Fishermen's Terminal, I found out that Blake had guessed right. One of the first stories I heard on the docks was about the one-legged man. His name was Gunnar. He had come to this country with the wave of immigrants after the Second World War. Starting out as a deckhand on a dragger, he moved up to renting a gillnetter and then bought one for himself. The only way anything was known about him was from his brother Harry. Arriving in Canada together, Harry did the talking for both of them. The only similarity between them was that they were both bachelors. The main difference was that while Gunnar was an absolute loner, Harry hung around with the gillnetters on D Float. It was through Harry that the story of how Gunnar had lost his leg came out.

One spring just before the season's first opening, Gunnar ordered a new exhaust pipe and muffler for his boat. The boat was primitive. The exhaust came up from the engine under the wheelhouse, along its back wall, and out through the roof. The engine ran hot and the original exhaust had been insulated with a guard over it to prevent burns.

The mechanic installed the new exhaust while Gunnar paced the dock, anxious to get started on his trip to the northern fishing grounds. Whether it was to save time or money, the insulation and guard over the exhaust were not installed. Gunnar paid off the mechanic and headed north the same day. As usual, he was travelling alone.

Harry, with a few of his cronies who always travelled together, started off a few hours later. Somewhere off Point Atkinson, they came upon Gunnar's boat with the engine running, slowly going around in circles. Approaching to investigate, they noticed an odd smell of roasting meat in the air, but no sign of Gunnar. Shouts and blasts of their whistles brought no reaction from the boat. Expecting the worst, Harry drew up to the circling boat and managed to tie up to it while underway.

Everything seemed to be in order on the decks and in the cockpit, but oddly enough, the wheelhouse door was closed. Sliding it open, he was hit with a wall of heat, engine fumes, and the roasting meat smell that was now a stench. Gunnar lay on his back on the wheelhouse floor. The stool he'd sat in at the helm was knocked over. Harry could feel heat radiating from the bare exhaust pipe from where he stood. His brother lay with one leg stretched out and the other bent at the knee, resting against the exhaust pipe. Despite his shock at realizing where the smell was coming from, Harry remembered to shut the engine down and pulled his brother out onto the deck where he lay like a dead man, but he was still breathing. While one of his cronies radioed the Coast Guard, Harry dragged his brother onto his boat and headed for Vancouver at top speed. The Coast Guard met him half way and took over from there. Harry's friends had followed him in, towing Gunnar's boat. After turning it over to the Coast Guard, they all resumed their journey north.

Gunnar was in a coma for a month. He woke up agitated and addled, his burned leg cut off. Harry came back from fishing early that fall to collect his brother from the hospital. Gunnar's head problems didn't improve, and he couldn't sleep because of nightmares, but he became calmer as time went on. He learned to get around on crutches. One day the following spring, Harry took him down to his boat. Any worries about how he would react to it were gone in the first few minutes. Once aboard, Gunnar had to be coaxed to get back off. Harry told his friends that when his brother was on his boat, he was as close to his old self as he would ever get— which wasn't close at all—but he seemed to remember how to run the boat and how to handle a gillnet.

Harry renewed his brother's salmon licence when he renewed his own. That spring, when his friends left for the northern fishing grounds, he didn't go with them. Instead, he waited with his brother for the salmon season to open locally. He used the time to insulate the exhaust, set up grab bars, and drop the boom on Gunnar's boat to help him get around. When the season opened, the two of them went out together on Gunnar's boat. After picking his first set, Gunnar, who still couldn't speak properly, let his brother know that he didn't need any more help. He wanted the boat to himself. Luckily he was a big man, Harry joked later, or his brother might have thrown him overboard in his rush to reclaim the boat for himself. The next day, Harry took his boat north for the remainder of the season, leaving his brother on his own.

The Coast Guard had kept Gunnar's boat at their dock for a few weeks then returned it to its moorage. They recommended insulating the exhaust system and placing a shield around it. There was no reference made by the Coast Guard or any other authority as to why Gunnar might have passed out to start the chain of events that led to his injuries, but Harry knew why it happened. The mechanic hadn't cut a hole in the gasket where the exhaust pipe connected to the muffler. Exhaust from the engine hadn't been able to get outside and had collected in the wheelhouse, overcoming his brother. While Gunnar was still recuperating, Harry went down to his boat and took the exhaust apart. He found the gasket had been properly cut out, but he also noticed that the edge of the cut looked fresh, not blackened by hours of engine exhaust passing through. It was obvious that the mechanic had realized his mistake and gone back to fix it after he heard about Gunnar. He could have easily been in and out in twenty minutes with no one the wiser.

Harry put the exhaust system back together and brooded for days about what to do next. He didn't think he'd get anywhere by going to the police or Coast Guard. They'd say it was an accident of Gunnar's making and wouldn't go after the mechanic. Harry could see why they wouldn't. The mechanic had made a mistake; it was as simple as that. There was no reason to think any malice was intended. If anything, Gunnar shouldn't have been too cheap to pay for insulation on the exhaust. He shouldn't have been running his boat with the door closed either. It was almost as if he'd been asking for trouble. There had been something like that, a self-destructive bent or a need to tempt fate, about his brother for as long as Harry could remember.

If this had been the old country, Harry knew he would have been expected to teach the mechanic a lesson for what he'd done to his brother. Here it was different, but at one point Harry had tailed the mechanic for a few days with a piece of rebar in his car, intending to break some bones. He was stopped for a light at a downtown intersection when a smartly dressed young couple crossed in front of him. She was Chinese and he was white. They were holding hands and laughing about something. Harry looked at himself in the rear-view mirror and saw an old man living in the past. When the light changed, he drove home, put the rebar back under his workbench, and got blind drunk. Part of the reason he drank was because he realized he'd have Gunnar on his hands for the rest of his life.

After that first night, I used to see Gunnar quite often. Like the other gillnetters, I tried to stay out of his way. He didn't care if he corked anyone when he set out his net, and couldn't be reasoned with if he did.

One evening, about five or six years after our first meeting, Gunnar left his usual fishing area for some reason, and set his net across the shipping lane. He may not have seen the freighter approaching. The freighter blew short blasts on its whistle as a warning, but, true to form, Gunnar ignored it. The freighter couldn't have stopped or swerved off even if the pilot had tried to. It ploughed into the middle of his net and kept going. Gunnar wasn't as lucky as I was when the tug hit my net that first night; his cork line didn't break. Still attached to the net, his boat was swept back against the side of the freighter and began to pound itself to kindling. The cork line finally tore free of the drum and his boat, badly damaged, spun away from the freighter. One of the gillnetters fishing nearby left his net and picked Gunnar up just as his boat began to sink.

The rescuer knew both brothers. He had radioed Harry as soon as he saw what was happening to Gunnar. Harry picked his net as fast as he could. Some of the fish that were hard to pick out he wrapped up on the drum. When he got to the scene he saw the freighter in the distance, still making for Vancouver. A few gillnet boats were idling near the spot where Gunnar's boat had gone down. A few bits of debris floated toward them and a faint oil slick was starting.

Rafting up to the rescuer's boat, Harry found his brother hunched over on the hatch cover, sobbing. It was the first time he'd seen his brother in such a state since they'd been children. Nothing he said calmed him, so he got a bottle of rye. He poured a good slug into a cup with some water and held it under his brother's nose. After looking at it for a while, Gunnar took the cup and gulped it down. He did the same with another. Little by little, Gunnar started communicating in the strange mixture of gibberish, disconnected words, and hand signs he had used since he'd lost his leg. He wanted to be taken to the debris patch.

Harry took his brother aboard his own boat so the rescuer could get on with fishing and make up for lost time. Harry watched his brother peering at the debris, afraid he might throw himself in, and then he realized what had happened. Gunnar's money was stashed aboard the boat. He had gone back to an old habit that Harry had warned him against so many times. When asked if it was true, Gunnar's expression of regret said it all. With the money gone, and no insurance on the boat, Harry knew it was the end for Gunnar. He gave him the rye bottle.

A while later the Coast Guard arrived. By the time they boarded the boat, Gunnar was passed out in the bunk. Harry answered their questions as best he could and kept fishing until the fishery ended the following morning. That same day he took Gunnar to see a lawyer. The settlement from the shipping company was enough to cover a year in the retirement home Harry found for his brother. A few years later, Harry quit fishing, sold his boat, and joined him. His friends on D Float didn't see any more of him after that.

|||||

After all the bad luck on my first night out, the encounter with the one-legged man was like a final warning not to tempt fate any further. Nothing had to be said. Blake and I tidied up the boat, washed down the decks with buckets of seawater, and headed for home. The catch for my first night gillnetting was nine sockeye and one small spring salmon. Anyone with a minimum of common sense would have realized that gill-netting wasn't for him and put his boat up for sale. As for me, I couldn't wait for the next opening.

The sea had calmed by the time we reached the freight-ers in the outside anchorages of English Bay. The Vancouver skyline, still with lights ablaze, guided us in from there. The wheelhouse windows were open and a warm breeze blew in. There was the smell of cedar bark from a passing scow, and then the scent of strong coffee as we opened our ther-moses. We ate our sandwiches with hands that smelled of fish scales, not talking much. That was my first run into Vancouver by sea at night. There have been many more since, all magical, but none quite like that one. It healed the night's disappointments: the net damage, the boat's seaworthiness, my shortcomings as a skipper, and the strange effect of the one-legged man. Even at that late hour there were lights on in some of the windows of the West End high-rises. There were still cars on Beach Avenue, the sight of their headlights and tail lights somehow comforting after the hours on dark water. As we got closer, the lights of the Burrard Bridge began to separate themselves from the high-rises and traffic lights of the waterfront streets. There were still a few cars on the bridge as we passed under it and turned toward the False Creek Fishermen's Terminal and home. It must have felt good for Blake, too, because he was grinning. He looked over at me and yelled over the sound of the engine: "Well, at least we didn't kill anybody!"

"Not yet anyway," I said, and we both laughed, never suspecting that someone would be out to kill me the next morning.

4

||| THE MORTAL INSULT |||

Early morning phone calls usually mean trouble, I thought as I heard the telephone ring. Valerie, who was already up getting ready for work, answered it. She said something and then hung up. I put my head under the pillow, hoping for a few more hours' sleep. A few minutes later the phone rang again. She answered it and said something else, but this time she didn't hang up. I knew it was trouble for sure.

She came over to the bed. "You awake?" she asked. "Listen, maybe you should take this call. I've already hung up on him and he just called back ..."

"What does he want?"

"Well, he's hard to understand, but I think he says he wants to kill you and sink your boat."

"Is that all? Okay, let's see if I can talk him out of it." I took the phone.

The man on the other end had an accent I hadn't heard before and was hard to understand. It didn't help that he was so enraged he was sputtering like Sylvester J. Pussycat on one of his cartoon tirades. Talking with him was impossible, so I hung up.

Valerie was hovering. "Is this something to do with last night?"

"Yeah, probably," I answered. "We tied up in another guy's spot."

"And that's why he wants to kill you?"

"Well, he had a chain across his spot and we moved it."

"You had a key?" she asked.

"No. I had Blake tear the chain out of its fastening."

"You what? Oh, so what are you going to do now?"

"Go and see what he's all about, I guess."

"I'll make you some sandwiches. Sounds like you'll need them."

I was out the door in twenty minutes. I showered, kissed Valerie goodbye, told her not to worry, and promised to call and let her know how things were going as soon as I could. In return, she gave me a thermos of coffee and a couple of fried-egg sandwiches. I was beginning to really love that woman.

The sandwiches were still warm as I wolfed them down, trying to comprehend how I could have been so stupid the previous night. Somehow it had seemed simpler to take the first convenient berth I saw instead of threading my way down to my assigned spot. In the dark I hadn't noticed the chain across it until the last minute. Taking leave of my senses completely, I had asked Blake to rip the end of the chain out of the timber it was fastened into. Seeing I was serious, he gingerly stepped off the *T.K.* onto the float, walked over to the end of the chain, ripped it out with a flourish, and tossed it aside. With the boat moored, we washed it down with a hose we found on the float, split the catch between us, and went home to bed.

Whether it had been the euphoria of surviving all the troubles that night, the strange effect of the one-legged gill-netter, or the anti-social behaviour Valerie said I sometimes demonstrated, what I did was wrong and I was prepared to answer for it. Driving into the parking lot, I was of two minds. I knew that I needed to make amends—but it was hard to stay contrite when my natural response to the violence threatened against me was to return fire.

Parking the car in my usual spot, I started down the ramp to the dock where I had committed the offence. As I got closer, I saw a large, odd-looking gillnet boat moored crossways at the end of the finger float where I'd tied up the *T.K.* The skipper, a man I'd noticed once or twice before on the docks, was standing on the bow of his boat with a pike pole in his hand. A knot of other gillnetters was gathered on the main float, watching him. Seeing all this in the light of day made me realize how my actions could be taken as a mortal insult by a certain kind of man. Stepping onto the finger float, I walked toward him, thinking an apology for taking over his spot might be a good starting point.

Before I could say a word, he yelled something, and drove the pike pole at my head. I dodged, grabbed its end just above the hook, and gave the pole a good yank. This jerked the man off balance and nearly threw him overboard. Recovering, he tried to rip the pike pole out of my grip. He was a big man, not tall, but thick and strong. I had some size too, and was a lot younger. I knew I could send him flying off his boat with another good yank, and so did he. He suddenly stopped pulling, and we stood there holding opposite ends of the pike pole, staring at each other.

"Behave yourself," I yelled at him, "or you'll be in the water! I'm going to let go of your pike pole now. Try anything, and by God you'll take a swim!"

I let go, ready for anything, but he just stood there silently, scowling at me.

"Look, I know I was wrong to take your spot last night," I said to him in what I thought was a reasonable voice. "I'll pay for the damage. Let me get my boat out of here and you can have your spot back. But you've got to move your boat first."

Locked in a stare with me, he didn't reply. Finally, after a comically long effort to outstare me, he started to move, his eyes not leaving mine. The spell was broken when he nearly tripped on his anchor winch and looked down to see what had happened. I may have laughed at this because he stiffened with rage and made as if to throw the pike pole at me, growling curses in his foreign language. The people on the dock muttered to each other. I took them to be friends of his, and turned to see if they had anything they wanted to say to me. They didn't, and merely looked amused at the standoff. One of them offered to help with my lines. The others helped push off my opponent's boat so I could back off the finger float. The fellow who helped with my lines suggested I try another spot at the end of the dock, and walked down to wait until I brought the *T.K.* around and help me tie up there.

"Watch that guy," he said when the boat was secure. "His name is Otto something or other, and he's a mean one. He'll take a swing as soon as look at you. That's not a guy you wanna cross. He's haywire."

The man doing the talking looked like an expert on the type. Even though it was a fine warm morning, he was dressed in a grey Stanfield's underwear top and thick brown woollen pants, two sizes larger than he needed. Red logger's suspenders kept the waistband of his pants up under his armpits. His pant legs were tucked into gumboots that were grey with dried fish scales. On his head was a Cowichan toque pulled down to his ears, making them stick out like jug handles. He grinned and squinted as he talked, saying his name was Harvey. His last name was something that sounded like "Houndstooth." Tall and thin with a stiff walk and breaking voice, he could have could have passed for Walter Brennan, the old movie actor.

"Thanks for the warning, Harvey," I said. "Nice toque, by the way. Looks warm."

"I used to bash my head on the radar and other stuff hanging off my wheelhouse ceiling before I got it. You got no idea. That's my boat there," he said, pointing to an old narrow-gutted troller with its hull painted in red lead primer that was moored just down the dock from where we were standing.

"Nice boat," I said. "Had it long?"

"Forever! Ya know, I once knocked myself out hitting my head on something in a rough sea. Luckily, that damn boat kept its course until I woke up. If it hadn't, chances are it woulda broached and gone over an' I wouldna been here tellin the story."

Harvey had endless stories, as I would find out. He told them with a childlike enthusiasm, speeding up, stopping for a quick breath, then speeding up again. Every spring he'd hire one of the young girls looking for work on the docks as a deckhand. Somehow it wasn't a surprise that none of them lasted a season. They didn't leave because he propositioned them, but because his constant chatter drove them crazy. Even from that first talk with him, I could see why.

Listening to Harvey, I watched the group of onlookers disperse. One of them hung back, and when I finally got clear of Harvey, he came over and introduced himself. His name was Pete, he said, and he was also new to gillnetting. Despite an age difference of about thirty years, he became one of my first friends on the dock. He walked me up to the wharfinger's office, where I arranged to leave my boat where I had just tied up. There wasn't anything wrong with the spot I already had on the other dock. I just didn't want Otto to think he'd run me off.

After calling Valerie to let her know I was still alive and well, my next efforts that day were to start putting what was left of my net together. I started by stripping it off the drum and piling it into a net cover to form a bundle. Moving the boat over to the main wharf, I used the hoist to raise the bundle off the boat and onto a wagon I'd seen other gillnetters using to move their nets around. I pulled the wagon over to an empty net rack and started to drape the net over it, imitating what I'd seen others do. A couple of gillnetters I recognized from the dock where I'd first moored stopped by to shake their heads at what had become of my net, and likely have a closer look at the fool who had crossed Otto. One of them showed me how to put the net on the rack more easily than I'd been doing, and mentioned that he knew a net-mender who might not be busy. I took the telephone number from him and, trying to sound casual, said I might give the net-mender a call later. I made the call as soon as he left, and the net-mender came the next day.

My first impression when he showed up was that he wasn't a net-mender at all. He moved with a bad limp and the left sleeve of his jacket was empty. The upper part of that arm seemed to be fused to his body, and he carried his hand across the front of his body with the fingers rigidly bent into a claw. He was wearing clothes you'd see in the evening on the Granville strip: a soft leather casual jacket, sharply creased trousers, and expensive Italian loafers. On his head was a narrow-brimmed fedora, which he wore tilted to one side in the manner of Frank Sinatra. If it weren't for the mending bench in his right hand and the equipment bag over his shoulder, I would have taken him for a nightclub tout.

When he got to where I was standing beside the rack, he introduced himself through the smoke of a cigarette in the corner of his mouth. "The name is Tak." He didn't ask for mine.

Turning to the net, he said, "Well, well, well. Whatever could have happened to this poor thing?"

"It was run over by a tug," I began, assuming he was speaking to me, but he wasn't.

"What'd you ever do to deserve this?" He ran his hand along the web hanging over one side of the rack. He was talking to the net.

"Hey, bud, you never told me it was this bad." He turned to me with an accusing look.

"Yeah, well ..." I shrugged. I didn't say anything more. He might have been setting me up for an outrageous price to do the work, or maybe he wasn't quite all there. Either way, he was convincing. After a long moment, he seemed about to say something, then turned on his heel and left. His mending bench and equipment bag were still where he'd dropped them. I took this for a sign that he'd be back. As he limped away, I could see that despite his appalling injuries, he was doing his best to swagger and appear cool. In a little while he came limping back with a small skein of web draped over his shoulder.

"I'll tell you what," he said. "I got this leftover web, same size and gauge, but a lighter colour. Should still work. It ain't enough to make a full-size net outta yer mess, but it'll be a helluva lot better than it was. You wannit?"

"Sure do!" On a second thought, I asked, "Can you tell me how much you figure it might cost? I'm kinda new at this stuff."

"A hunnert'n fifty, cash. It'll be done in about three hours."

A hundred and fifty dollars was about forty sockeye in those days. It didn't seem cheap, but forty sockeye could easily be caught in one set, or so I was told. My best set—my only set—up to that point was five, and I wasn't even sure if they were all sockeye.

"Okay, go ahead," I told him.

"But ya unnerstan, you ain't gonna have a full net at the end of all this, don't ya?"

"I do. How long of one do you think I'll end up with, anyway?"

"I dunno, kid, maybe a hunnert and eighty fathoms if yer lucky, maybe less."

"That's better than I expected." I helped him line up the net the way he wanted it on the rack, and hung around, hoping to learn something about how mending was done. He started by snipping away huge sections of torn web using curiously shaped scissors that hung from his neck on a leather cord. When I asked if I could help in any way, he curtly refused, giving me the feeling he wished I'd go away and let him work.

Watching him was so fascinating I didn't want to leave. He used his claw hand to keep tension on sections of net when he was snipping and when he was stitching in panels, or simply mending holes, a cigarette in his mouth the whole time. When one was smoked to the butt, he'd spit it out and then take a fresh one out of a pack in the inside of his jacket and light it with a Zippo lighter. He did all this with his right hand, holding the part of the net he was working on with his left. He was so deft, it took just a few seconds each time. Using the Italian loafer on his good foot, he crushed the smoldering butts and scraped them into a little pile under the mending bench. Between lighting cigarettes, his right hand flew about the net so quickly it was a blur. Learning something from him that I could make my clumsy hands do later looked impossible. He glanced at me with a half-smile now and then as he worked. I suspected he was showing off for my benefit. Given the shape he was in, I didn't grudge him that at all. There was even a swagger in the way he handled a mending needle, and that was something to admire.

He didn't say anything until he'd gone through four cigarettes. Then he asked, "You wanna pass me another pack of cigs? They're in my bag under the needles."

There were five or six packs in the bag. I got one out, tore off the cellophane wrapper, and handed it to him.

"Thanks, kid," he said. "You smoke?"

"Nah, never started."

"Why not? Scared?" he grinned as he said it.

"Scared? Nah, they just made me sick," I replied.

"Ya shoulda stuck to it. Ya coulda been like me." He was still grinning, showing yellow teeth. I couldn't tell if he was mocking himself or me.

"I guess persistence isn't my long suit."

"Hah!" he snorted. "Good answer. Very diplomatic." He went back to concentrating on his work, and I hoped he'd leave it there, but he didn't. A few minutes later he said, "So how long you been fishin?"

"Six hours, maybe a bit less."

"What?" he looked up in surprise, his cool demeanour slipping a little.

"You heard right."

"No shit. And you mangled your net this bad!" He laughed.

"Well, it does take a certain talent."

He laughed again. "Man," he said, "my first opening I caught more socks than my old man, and not a tear in the net. Of course, I'd been fishing with him and my uncles since I was a kid, before the war."

I didn't know what to say next. He was Japanese. His family must have been among the people who had been moved into camps during the war, the boats owned by his father and uncle confiscated.

Reading my mind, he went on. "Yeah, we were all sent to Greenwood. Never got our stuff back. We didn't get back to the coast till '52."

I couldn't understand why he was telling me this, or why he said it so calmly. I couldn't imagine the rage I'd feel if that had happened to me. He kept working, squinting through the smoke of his cigarette as if nothing had been said. Not knowing how to respond, I blurted out the first thing on my mind.

"How did you get hurt?"

"Wanna know, huh? Well, at least you're honest enough to ask straight out." After thinking for a while, he said, "I blew up my boat with me in it. Port Hardy, it was. Gas boat, first cigarette in the morning, and kablam! Blew me through the side of the boat and thirty feet out in the water. Lucky it did, or I would have fried in the fire."

I stared at him. He told the story as if it had happened to someone else.

"Was it a gas leak?" I asked, thinking how my own boat had smelled of gasoline the other night when I couldn't get the engine started.

"More'n likely. That an' these cigareets. You're lucky you never smoked, kid."

"I guess you never went back to fishing after that."

"Naw, too crippled up. I stick ta net mendin'. Safer for a guy like me."

He went quiet after that. I was still stunned by the story he'd told me and couldn't think of ways to keep him talking. Chances were he wouldn't have anyway. He was no Harvey Houndstooth with everything on the surface and ready to blab away. I was surprised he'd told me about how he'd been hurt. I was even more surprised when I tried to pay him after he was done with my net. He refused the hundred and fifty, saying it was too much. Half that would do, he said. When I insisted, he took a hundred dollars and pushed the rest down my shirt pocket.

"Keep it, kid," he said. "I make more than enough at this racket. You need it more than me."

Tak had done a great job on the net, but there was more damage done every opening. There were ragged holes left by dogfish and tears from logs and other debris in the water. Most of the damage was caused by dogfish. They swam into the net with their mouth open and shredded anything that touched their deceptively sharp little teeth. Even a small dog-fish could chew a hole in the net the size of a manhole cover. It was obvious that getting Tak or someone else to mend my net each time was a money loser. I had to learn how to do it myself, but I needed a mentor—a patient one, judging from my clumsy attempts at net mending so far. I kept an ear out for someone appropriate but I wasn't having any luck.

That may have been because all my luck had been spent landing my deckhand. After the first night with Blake, Valerie had come out for the remaining openings that year and quickly made herself into an able deckhand. From pulling dogfish and hake out of the net to pumping out the bilges with the sheet metal deck pump, she did her share of the work with grace and stamina. If it hadn't been for her, I might have given up on the whole idea of gillnetting after some of the nights that engine problems, tide rips, high winds, or some-times all three made miserable. It wasn't a surprise when, after picking our last set of the year, she said she couldn't wait for the season to begin the following year.

5

THE MAN WITH
||| THE BORGWARD ISABELLA |||

From time to time, I passed Otto on the float. For the first few weeks after our set-to, he went by muttering what I took to be curses in that foreign language of his. I replied with a few of my own in English. One evening he merely brushed past with a scowl, and I gave him one of my own in return.

Scowling became our usual greeting until an afternoon a few days into the new year, a little over four months after the day he'd threatened to kill me. I had gone down to the dock to check on the *T.K.* and was hurrying along just as he stepped up from his finger float to the dock. It was raining hard and I had my head down. I just avoided crashing into someone at the last second. Before quite realizing who it was, I apologized.

"Tenk you. Heppy New Year," he replied in his thick accent, with what I thought was a faint smile.

I was so surprised that we were past each other before I could reply. From the glimpse I had, he seemed to be nattily dressed in a tan overcoat and dark green fedora. I had the impression he was wearing an ascot. From his greeting and his clothes, I took it he was still celebrating the new year. Curiously, I had thought of him as someone who didn't celebrate much of anything. He was separated from his wife, according to Harry Houndstooth, and lived by himself with only a couple of dogs for company. From that I had pictured him to be some kind of misanthrope.

In contrast to this, Rudy, a troller I was getting to know on my new dock, told me that Otto was a European-trained tool and die maker. He had a full workshop with a metal lathe in his basement and there wasn't anything he couldn't make out of metal. He was also a beekeeper, had fruit trees on his property, and kept a large garden. If true, that made him more interesting, but still, in my mind, a misanthrope. The New Year's encounter started to change that.

Somewhere about the first week of February, Otto and I exchanged the few words that didn't get spoken in our last encounter. A week later he invited me for coffee on his boat. By then I had been inside enough gillnet boats to know what they usually looked like. Otto's was completely different from any I'd seen, larger for one thing, and much less in the marine tradition. It was more like a summer cottage than a commercial fishboat. We had our coffee at his galley table, sitting on chrome kitchen chairs straight out of the '50s. The table had an Arborite top in a grey pattern like one I remembered from our kitchen when I was a boy. His galley stove looked like it came from a farmhouse and the cupboards could have been salvaged from a suburban bungalow.

To go with the coffee, Otto put out a plate of oatmeal cookies, a bowl of butter, and a jar of honey. The cookies tasted best with butter and honey, he said. I tried some and had to agree, if only because the cookies were so old they tasted like particleboard. The honey was delicious, amber in colour, and smelling of the flowers it had been made from. When I complimented him on it, he flushed with pride and began to tell me about his bees and their amazing abilities. For instance, they had memories that lasted three days. He knew this because they'd stung him when he came close to their hives for the first three days after he took their honey-combs, but on the fourth day they left him alone. Bees were the most beneficial of creatures, he said; even their stings were useful because they prevented arthritis. He told me all this with a guileless wonder; it was hard to believe this was the same man who had gone for my eyes with a pike pole a few months earlier.

A day or two after we'd had coffee, I was in the parking lot getting something out of the truck when I saw Otto approaching. He was driving a car I'd never seen before, a coupe that reminded me of a plump grey pigeon at first glance. I'd usually seen him driving a black station wagon, a Borgward, which was unusual but nothing to draw a second look. This car did. I watched him inch the car into a parking space at the speed of an ocean liner easing into its berth. From the side, the car looked a little leaner than a pigeon, and oddly stylish. It had a high window line, rounded windows, smallish wheel wells, and thin tires. In a way, it resembled a scaled-down early 1950s Mercury coupe, a car often custom-ized and souped up by hot-rodders. This one was stock to the point that its grey paint had probably never been exposed to Simoniz. Its badges said "Borgward Isabella," a name that was charmingly apt.

It took Otto a while to get out of the car. Before opening the door, he set the emergency brake and checked to see that the windows were rolled up, the headlights were off, and that he hadn't left the key in the ignition. When all was in order, he opened the door, being careful it didn't touch the car beside him. Finally, he put one foot onto the pavement, then the other. He had to tilt his head to avoid the doorframe so as not to dent his hat, the same one he was wearing when our relationship began to thaw. When he was finally out of the car and turned toward me, I had to whistle. The rest of his attire did justice to the hat. Under a Harris Tweed sports jacket that looked like a size fifty (and was tight on him) was a pale yellow shirt and a maroon ascot. Pearl-grey flannel pants with a sharp crease and highly polished brogans that looked to be about size fourteen completed his outfit. He beamed when I whistled.

"Otto, you look fantastic! You getting married or what?"

"No, no, vonce enough," he smiled. "I go visit lady vriend. Ve hef lunch togedder today."

"Wow, lucky lady," I said.

"Ya, she lucky. I makem heppy, " he said with a roguish smile that was surprising to see on his normally dour face. "I be home late today."

"Well, I hope you have a good time. By the way, nice car."

"Tenk you. Oh, you like my sport car, ya? I use for visitink ladies only."

We walked down to our boats together, talking about nothing in particular. Twenty minutes later I saw him go back up the dock, turning heads as he went. I didn't see him again until a few days later, dressed in his work clothes, driving the station wagon, and all business.

I asked him how his date went, but he didn't understand what I meant at first. Then he said: "Oh, not so goot. She too oldt. I tink time for new model, maybe."

I wondered how long he'd had the old model, and how long it would take him to find a new one, but didn't ask. Something told me he already had the next model in mind. He drove the station wagon for a few weeks after that, and didn't mention anything about new models.

He invited me over for coffee again, and I reciprocated a few days later by inviting him aboard the *T.K.* It didn't start well. As he stepped over the rail, his weight threw the boat into such a roll that the coffee pot nearly flew off the stove, and hot coffee shot out of the spout, splashing everywhere. I hadn't realized how thick and heavy a man he was until he tried to squeeze down into the galley. He was plainly uncomfortable there, and we ended up having our coffee sitting out on the hatch cover. It was a chilly day and our coffee turned cold in a few minutes. Otto didn't seem to mind the chill, but from then on we had coffee on his boat.

One day soon afterwards, he showed me more of his boat. Beamy and more than forty feet long, it looked like the work of a backyard builder, one more familiar with barges than boats. The builder must have had a sense of humour because he'd named his creation *Joker Too*. Otto had owned the boat for years, and had made many "improvements," as he called them. He'd started in the fo'c'sle, lining it with varnished tongue-and-groove cedar, panelling to give it a light Scandinavian look. It was surprisingly roomy with a wide bunk and built-in cabinets. It was so unlike his own persona that I suspected that he'd built it with his wife in mind before their marriage went bad.

The most interesting part of the boat was the engine room. The original gasoline engine had been replaced with a four-cylinder Bolinder diesel. It was a brand I hadn't heard of, but one that Otto knew from Europe. He had to admit his boat was a little underpowered and parts were hard to come by, but that was minor when compared to how cheap it was to run. Besides, he didn't like travelling too fast, he said, or he'd miss the scenery. The European tool- and die-maker training Rudy had told me about was evident in the custom-made engine mounts, drive-shaft couplings, power take-offs to various pumps, and the shaft steering system—to name just the first things that caught my eye. There were work-benches on each side of the engine, tucked against fuel and water tanks, with tool drawers underneath. Other tools were neatly clipped to supporting frames to keep them secure in heavy seas. Of special interest to me, after my efforts to fix a balky engine on my boat by flashlight, were the neatly made shielded work lights in critical areas.

After our tour of the engine room, we climbed up to the main deck where Otto took me over to show off the helm he had built into the port side. It had a large traditional wheel of varnished mahogany mounted below a dashboard big enough for spreading out charts. A three-paned wind-shield across the front of the cabin and large side windows provided a great sweep of visibility from the helm. The col-lection of gauges and controls around the wheel was much more impressive than any I had seen on other boats. Every gauge and control was backed up with a spare in case one failed. Although he'd never had to go to any of the spares, he said they were there if need be. This need for spares, as I was beginning to see, was one of Otto's dominant traits.

He insisted I try out the helm seat. It was salvaged from a top-of-the-line Mercedes-Benz and had a built-in heater. Otto had installed his own recliner controls and wired it so the heater worked. It was the first time I'd been in a heated seat, or even knew such a thing existed, and I was envious. Smiling ruefully, he said he was really thinking about discon-necting the heater because it made him fall asleep in the chair instead of keeping a sharp eye on his net. In later years when Valerie and I fished near him, we'd often see his net pulled out into a straight line behind his boat, and know that he still hadn't disconnected the heater.

A week after touring his boat, I received an invitation to visit him at his house. It was in the form of a crisply folded piece of paper with his address and the time he expected me to arrive neatly printed on it. He lived on the North Shore on a street of pleasant suburban houses with lawns stretching down to the sidewalk. His house was behind a tall hedge of scrubby firs and hollies that had been woven through with wire fencing and rods of reinforcing steel. The only way in was a narrow asphalt driveway, which was barred by seven-foot-tall plywood-and-steel gates that were painted a dull brown. There was a battered mailbox perched on a gate post, and rusty numerals nailed to a tree trunk faintly confirmed the address. I parked the truck on some unkempt grass in front of the hedge and got out. I hadn't seen the real thing, but the scene somehow made me think of standing in front of the Berlin Wall.

Otto was behind the gate waiting for me. A growling black dog sniffed me up and down as I was let in. Before closing and locking the gate behind me, Otto looked up and down the street as if he was expecting trouble. The dog didn't seem interested in what was going on outside the gate. He had stopped growling, but sat on the driveway a few feet away from me, watching as I looked over the yard. It was wide and deep, made up of two generous city lots. A two-storey house stood at the end of the driveway, the entrance to its carport screened off by a green tarp. The Borgward Isabella and the station wagon were parked in front of it. Two other Borgwards, apparently kept for spare parts, were under some flowering plums beside the driveway. Behind the house, partially hidden behind stands of tall flowers, were several outbuildings. In various places around the yard were fruit trees, berry bushes, a vegetable garden, lawns, beehives, and a pond glinting in the sun behind a stand of bamboo. It was "blossom time" as Otto called it, and flowers and trees were blooming everywhere, filling the air with a sweet scent that was a sharp contrast to the ominous street front of his property.

Otto led me around his yard, pointing out the different plants and trees, calling most of them by their English name, and telling me how he'd acquired them. Not one sounded like it had been bought; most seemed to have been salvaged from properties where old houses were being demolished and the existing plants were there for the taking. The dog followed, sniffing at my heels and growling from time to time. We stopped beside a small table and a couple of wrought iron chairs set up beside the pond. Otto invited me to sit while he went into the house to prepare tea. He refused my offer to help, so I sat and looked around while the dog crouched on his haunches a little distance away and watched me. There was a cover of expanded metal mesh painted the same colour as the gates protecting the pond from what I took to be raccoons. Now and then there would be a glimpse of a golden koi beneath it. Bees were buzzing in the flowers all around the pond and it was so peaceful I expected the dog to doze, but he didn't take his eyes off me until his master came back with tea, cookies, butter, and honey on a large tray.

With the tea poured, Otto began to talk. He wanted to know more about me and where my parents were from. I had the feeling it was important for him to know, as if it helped peg me in his estimation. When I told him, he nodded as if confirming a hunch. He had lifted weights when he was a teenager, he said, and one of his heroes was George Hackenschmidt, a strongman he believed was from the same stock as my parents. I vaguely recalled seeing a picture of the man lifting a lawn roller or something over his head when he was in his seventies.

"I'm glad to hear he's one of ours."

"Maybe even a relative," said Otto, beaming at me with delight.

Otto had an interesting face, a lot like Nikita Khrushchev's in the way it changed from angry to happy. He looked exactly like the famous shot of Khrushchev banging his shoe on the United Nations table when he was enraged, as I'd found that morning he'd gone for my eyes with the pike pole. But when he was smiling the way he was in his garden, it was impossible not to like him and feel the warmth of the moment. I'd once heard that people are born with wells of opposing emotions that match each other in size. Those capable of the greatest hate are capable of the greatest love and so forth. If so, Otto was a prime example. He was a man of extremes if there ever was one.

Beginning to talk about himself, he told me he had been five when his father died and he didn't have any real memories of him. It was just after the First World War and people all around were dying of influenza. Being an only child with no relatives to look after him, or other children nearby to play with, he grew up alone. His mother had to work every day, leaving early in the morning and getting back late at night. Being used to doing things his own way, he got into a lot of fights when he was older. He lost a few at first, but he practised and put on a few pounds; after that he didn't lose any.

While in his late teens, Otto shipped out on a freighter that operated mostly in tropical waters. He remembered many of the ports with disgust. It was in one of them that he had his first beer. It turned out to be the last time he drank alcohol because it made him sick and gave him a headache. He had also noticed how fast money flew away in the sailors' bars, and knew they weren't for him. The bars and pubs here were no different, he thought, although he'd never been in one to find out.

When he left his ship, he went back to his hometown and learned the tool- and die-making trade. He got his papers, found a job, and bought a house. In his spare time, he started a taxi business. The Nazis invaded soon after the Second World War started, and he left again, this time for good. He was married by then and had a son. The three of them sailed to Sweden, crossing the Baltic on a small overloaded boat with an engine that Otto had to nurse along. Their reception in Sweden made him realize there was no future for his family there, so they came to Canada in the wave of refugees of the early '50s, ending up in Toronto. Leaving his wife and son in the train station when they arrived, he spent his first day there looking for a job and a place to stay. He found both, and they lived in Toronto but didn't settle in. When he had saved enough, he bought a 1948 straight-eight Pontiac and they drove across the continent to Vancouver. He still had the same car. It was in a garage behind his carport, buried under a lot of stuff, but he thought he could get it running again someday.

After renting in Vancouver for a couple of years, working two jobs and saving every penny, Otto had enough money to buy the house we were sitting beside for cash. The first time he'd borrowed money was when he and his wife separated so he could buy her out of her share of the house. By then he'd bought the *Joker Too*, and his first years fishing had been good. Working two jobs in the off-season, he paid off the loan in a few years. It was like being let out of jail, he said. Now he had money in the bank and didn't owe "any penny" to anyone.

He and his wife had been in a virtual state of war before she left, and she'd tried sniping at him through their countrymen afterwards. There had been vague threats against him, which was why he kept his gate locked and a dog in the yard. Every time he went down to his boat, he checked for bombs. Now that he was getting old, he wanted nothing more than to be left alone to a peaceful life.

Peace, to Otto, was a relative term. It sounded like he was in a simmering campaign of minor sabotage against his neighbour to the east. The neighbour had been a friend of his wife, and when she left, he'd thrown pieces of meat laced with rat poison over the fence for Otto's two dogs to eat. Luckily the older dog was smart enough not to touch the meat, and taught the younger dog not to as well. In return, Otto had built a seven-foot-high wooden fence between their two properties and planted trees to block his neighbour's afternoon sun. From time to time, Otto threw short lengths of wire over the fence into his neighbour's yard to foul the blades of his lawn mower when he cut the grass. Otto also trained his dogs to bark whenever they heard the neighbour in his yard to spoil his enjoyment of it. Now that the older dog was dead, the younger dog wasn't as attentive to this, much to Otto's disgust.

Over the years there had been an argument or two with the other neighbours around him, but a sort of détente had been reached. Otto made annual peace offerings to them in the form of freshly caught sockeye. In return, they tolerated his unusual hedge on their otherwise pretty street, and his dog when it barked at the eastern neighbour. He'd lived through states of siege from city officials for alleged building violations, unlicensed dogs, and unsightly premises by refusing to allow them onto his property. They had since stopped trying.

Otto still missed his older dog, now buried in his raspberry patch. He'd named him Ivanovitch, and remembered fondly how he'd kill raccoons and attack without warning if anybody ventured onto his property. His surviving dog, Laban, the one who was keeping his eyes on me, was not nearly mean enough in Otto's view. The next time I visited, he wanted me to twist Laban's tail to make him more aggressive to strangers. I did try it once, but only half-heartedly. After that, Laban wouldn't let me near him.

A few visits later, Otto told me I was welcome to let myself in the gate. He showed me how to reach in through a small opening for the key to unlock it. Laban was always there when I let myself in. I told Otto what a good watchdog he was, expecting he'd be pleased to hear it. Instead, he shook his head sadly and said Laban was nothing but a playboy and a phony. When Ivanovitch was alive, the whole neighbourhood was afraid of him and raccoons getting at his koi were never a worry. Since Laban's death, Otto had had to chase Jehovah's Witnesses from his gate and the neighbour's cat from his garden. He never had to do these things when there was a real dog in the yard. Now, even with those ugly screens over the pond, the koi kept disappearing. Laban ate the same food he'd given Ivanovitch: oatmeal boiled with meat cuttings from the Safeway dumpster. He added a little raccoon meat when he could, but that was becoming rare with Laban being so slack. He hadn't learned a thing from Ivanovitch and he was lucky Otto put up with him.

One day that spring, Otto mentioned that his chimney was leaking. He had a steeply sloping roof, and I knew he was worried about trying to get up there himself. That following Saturday I dropped over in my running shoes and said I'd have a look. He protested at first, but when he saw I was serious, he relented. He had a supply of ladders, as he did with most things, but, as usual, there was something wrong with each of them. We lashed the two best ones together and I started up. The roll roofing was old, but still serviceable, and gave a good grip to my running shoes. I finished the job, a simple re-caulk, added a few more roofing nails around the chimney flashing, and an hour later we were sitting by the koi pond with our jackets off in the warm sun.

"Tenks for help," he said. "You vas climbink around my roof like leetel bird."

"You're welcome," I replied. "Anytime."

"How your nets?" he asked. "You learn anyt'ink from Yapanese guy?"

"Not much, he's too fast for me."

"I slower. I teach you."

"Well, thanks, Otto, that would be great, but you don't have to," I began.

"For sure I haff to! Vhy not?" he interrupted. "You help me, I help you. How many nets you haff?"

"Only the one."

"Vhat! Only von?" he almost shouted in his surprise. "No goot, you need more! I teach you net hangink too! Don't vorry, everytink you need is here."

Among his many oddities, Otto didn't trust the fishing companies with his nets, and kept them at home. I had noticed on my previous visits that his carport was set up like a net loft. My net was there the following Saturday. From then on until fishing started that summer, we worked on our nets together every weekend and many days in between.

One of Otto's strengths was his endless patience, even with a slow learner like me. Although his pinkie finger was the size of my thumb, he showed me how to tie knots that were small and tight, and how to make hangings so even they might have been turned out by a machine. While we worked, he told me stories about fishing in exotic-sounding places like Milbanke Sound, Bella Bella, and Namu, and narrow escapes in places like Queen Charlotte Sound, and a place that sounded like "the Yuca-toss." All the hanging twine, corks, cork line, and lead line that I needed, he kept finding among his spares. The only thing I had to pay for was web, and even that he wangled a good deal on from one of the suppliers who seemed to wince from the pain of dealing with Otto on previous occasions. By the time the season opened, my first net had been mended and extended, and I had a couple of new ones in my arsenal.

Our net-mending sessions had become something I looked forward to every week. In addition to his stories about fishing, he began to tell me about his new interest in garage sales. He had started going to them with another old gillnetter who had a boat almost as unique as the *Joker Too*. It sounded like he never left one without buying something. Every time I came over, he would show me the latest things he'd bought, marvelling at how little he paid, and wondering how people could part with such good stuff so readily. Clocks were his favourite, especially the wind-up kind. Some days he'd come home with two or three. The walls of his dining area and living room became covered with them, not many keeping the same time, but all ticking away. Piles of his other purchases had started to grow in the basement and the upstairs rooms of his house. The worst of it was that he wasn't piling this stuff into empty rooms; it was going on top of his collections of spares and extra parts to everything imaginable that had already half-filled these spaces. When I pointed out that there soon wouldn't be room for him in his house if he kept this up, he laughed at himself and said I was right, but it didn't sound like he was intending to stop his garage sale jaunts any time soon.

The one part of his house safe from this onslaught was his workshop. His tools numbered in the many hundreds, from the smallest of hand tools like optometrists' screwdrivers to a large metal-cutting lathe. Somewhere along the way he'd taken the time to designate a place for every one of them. As he'd added to his collection over the years, he'd made more shelves and longer hooks, but kept to his system. He seemed to be resisting the urge to pile up more of his garage sale loot anywhere near his workshop, almost as if realizing that if he began to do so, he'd lose all control of his garage sale habit.

When I took Valerie to Otto's house with me for the first time, she wasn't surprised by what she saw. She said it was a natural reaction to having grown up fatherless with a mother who had to be away every day so they could survive. Having lost everything in the war didn't help, nor did the bitter separation from his wife. People who had survived an existence like this often became hoarders, she explained, and Otto, as disciplined as he was in every other aspect of his life, couldn't control this.

One other aspect of his life he never quite seemed to control was his lady friends. His current belle was Regina, a fifty- or sixtyish refined widow from his home country who called him her "barbar," which I took to mean "barbarian." Shortly before fishing started, Valerie and I were invited to join Otto at her home in the west side of Vancouver for a send-off for our trip north. She co-hosted the gathering with her sister Stephania. They greeted us in low-cut evening gowns fit for a ballroom in Vienna, or more likely Copenhagen, where Regina said she'd lived most of her life. The table setting was fit for nobility with florid china, sparkling crystal, and gleaming silverware. We had brought a large bouquet of cut flowers, but the arrangement on the table made ours look paltry. The Champagne was Mumm, the wine was French, the vodka was Polish, and there was caviar to start. The meal was elaborate but overdone, as if the sisters weren't used to cooking, or the caterer had got the time wrong. The food was accompanied by many sauces, each in a delicate china dish, which we passed around to each other. The dishes nearly disappeared in Otto's hands as they were handed to him. I could see him flush and begin to sweat as each dish was passed his way. Perhaps wanting to make Otto more comfortable, Stephania mentioned that they were used to having waiters assist at dinner, but sadly, that wasn't done in this country.

After dinner, the sisters went to the piano. Regina played and Stephania sang. They named each piece and the composer before starting, and sang in the language of their origin. Stephania had a trained voice that wavered a little in the high notes, and her sister played confidently without sheet music. We clapped at the end of each song, and they did a gracious little bow, as if they'd been doing this all their lives. They asked if we had any requests, or if Valerie and I knew any songs that we could sing for them. Foolishly, I told them the only songs I knew weren't meant for mixed company. They tittered at this and tried to get me up to the piano, with Stephania taking me by the hand as encouragement. I finally talked them out of the idea and she reluctantly let my hand go, but not before giving it a loving caress. As she went back to her place at the piano, she gave me a well-practised coy glance out of the corner of her eyes that got me a sharp jab from Valerie. It turned out the sisters knew a few songs of their own that might not have been meant for mixed company by our standards, but must have been quite acceptable in the European circles they were used to. They were up-tempo songs they encouraged us to clap our hands to, while laughing uproariously at Otto, who, obviously understanding the lyrics, grinned wickedly and blushed to bursting at the same time.

Fuelled by the wine and vodka, the sisters were definitely getting friskier as the evening went on, even moving some of the furniture aside to dance. I caught Otto's attention and made a sign to my watch, letting him know it was time we left. He nodded, with a glint in his eye, laying to rest my worry that he'd be put off by the prospect of spending the rest of the evening with the two women. Valerie and I made our escape after indignant refusals of our offer to help with the dishes and pleas to stay longer. We thanked them for the lovely evening and endured lingering hugs before making it to the door. As we left, there was a squeal and a giggle from Stephania. Otto was right behind her, and from his wink I suspected he'd pinched her and that the party would liven up after we left.

The next morning Otto didn't turn up at his boat until noon. He arrived in the clothes he'd worn the night before, his hat askew and his ascot thrown over his collar.

"Oh, momma," he said with a tired grin. "All night no escape. We need to go fishink before they catch me again."

6

||| THE FISH CAMP |||

The False Creek Fishermen's Terminal had been a quiet place over the winter. Most days, the wharfingers making their rounds were the only people moving on the floats. But as salmon season approached, skippers who hadn't seen their boats for months began to show up every day. They eased into the fishing season by having coffee with their friends and catching up on a winter's worth of gossip. They talked about where they'd been for their holidays, complained about what they were paid for salmon compared to the price in the stores, and discussed their expectations for the coming year. It took some of them a couple of days and others longer, but eventually each one of them stopped talking and got working on their boats. The owners of wooden boats, who were still in the majority, started earlier on the yearly ritual of scraping and painting their vessels. Owners of newer boats built of fibreglass and sometimes aluminum, being free of much of that work, started later. Whether old or new, all the boats needed pressure washing and anti-fouling paint. The wisest skippers were the earliest on the tidal grids at the Fishermen's Terminal, or the ways at the nearby marinas. The *T.K.* was one of the last ones up. My excuse was that I still worked full-time at the architectural office.

By then, some of the boats were already leaving for their season. The first to go were the West Coast trollers. They were locally built and beautifully maintained by their proud skippers. Mostly painted white with grey or buff trim, they had varnished bright work, oiled decks, and gleaming stainless steel fittings. Some of those boats dated back to the 1920s, a few even earlier. They were all well over forty feet in length with broad-shouldered prows, tapering sheer lines, and square sterns with rounded corners. With their tall masts, even taller trolling polls, and intricate rigging, they were the best-looking fishing vessels on the coast. Everyone stopped what they were doing to watch them go by.

Next out, having the farthest to go, were the Nass and Skeena gillnetters, followed by those bound for Caamaño Sound, Milbanke Sound, Bella Bella, Namu, and Hakai Pass. These were names that inflamed the imagination, especially after a winter of hearing Otto's stories about fishing in those places. These gillnetters were also formidable vessels. All were shiny with new paint, bristling with aerials and radar units, and many gave off the throaty rumble of diesel engines as they glided away from their berths for the season's fishing.

The *T.K.*, despite my work, looked small and fragile by comparison. It was spruced up, though, in fresh white paint with dark green trim and new copper paint on the bottom. Over the winter I had extended the wheelhouse so it could fit two people comfortably (more or less), cleaned up the trunk cabin, and built a larger bunk. In spite of these efforts, the kindest word to describe the *T.K.* was "spartan."

We were heading north without an oil stove, a proper head, a VHF radio, a depth sounder, or a marine compass on the boat. Valerie and I had fished together enough times the previous fall to have found ways of compensating for their lack. A Coleman camp stove served for cooking and a galvanized bucket was our head. I had also installed a CB radio, or Mickey Mouse as the gillnetters called it, and made a depth sounder out of a line marked in fathoms with a lead weight on the bottom. An old Boy Scout compass I'd used in the bush since I was about twelve was taped onto the dashboard. Since our fishing was going to be in sheltered waters, some narrower than the lakes I was used to, I wasn't worried about heading out with the equipment we had.

We were hoping to make it to Rivers Inlet, a place that I'd heard fabulous stories about even before starting commercial fishing. We were going to travel with Otto. To prepare us for the trip, he told us stories about what to expect. The big obstacle in getting to Rivers Inlet, he said, was crossing Queen Charlotte Sound, with its full exposure to the open Pacific. Otto, who had travelled the globe as a deep-sea sailor when he was a young man, said that the swells there were as large as any he'd seen on his voyages. Some years crossing the Sound, he'd passed boats that didn't make it and were left adrift, semi-submerged with water lapping at their wheelhouse windows. These were the wooden boats—others had gone to the bottom. Valerie and I looked at each other when he said this, imagining the *T.K.* coming to a similar end.

Perhaps noticing the look between us, Otto finished his story by saying we'd be wise to wait and see how well the *T.K.* handled the trip up to that point before deciding whether to cross the Sound. If things didn't look good, he suggested we fish the Goletas Channel off Port Hardy on the northern end of Vancouver Island. He knew the area well and said it could have good fishing in July, although we'd have to be careful of the winds funnelling down the channel from the Pacific. Luckily there were islands to duck behind for shelter. There was also Hardy Bay and a fish camp he called Duval Point.

We finally left Vancouver on a fine Sunday morning at the end of June, well after the trollers and northern gillnetters had departed. The trip went well for an hour. We were off the southeast point of Bowen Island when the Gray Marine started to clatter and lose power, and finally stopped running.

"At least it's daylight and it's a calm sea, not like that first time it broke down," I said to Valerie as I climbed down to see what was wrong. "This shouldn't take long."

Otto stood by in the *Joker Too* as I crawled around the engine I was fast growing to hate. An hour later, I still hadn't found the problem, and the wind was coming up. Otto took us in tow and we sheltered in a small unnamed cove on the east side of Bowen Island opposite Horseshoe Bay. I finally found the problem: burned breaker points. And the spares I had bought didn't fit.

It was still blowing, but Otto cheerfully towed us back into Vancouver to find new ones. Regular marine supply stores didn't carry the points I needed because the engine was so old, but I had found an industrial lift truck repair shop that did. Luckily, it stayed open late. Pete, who wasn't going north that year, was on his boat smoking one of his ropey cigars and gave us a lift home. I took my car and raced out to the shop before it closed. Valerie sensibly stayed behind and baked bread. We got back to the boat by midnight and went to bed.

The next morning, Monday, we had coffee and Valerie's bread for breakfast on Otto's boat. With the weather still blowing and more forecast to come, we decided to postpone leaving until the next day. Otto went home to tend to his bees, Valerie worked on her thesis, and I installed the breaker points. Once again, the Gray Marine started up and ran as if nothing had happened.

Valerie had boarded Fred out to a kennel that she liked and we had no reason to go back to the apartment. For the first time in our relationship, we stayed aboard together for the whole day. Even with the limitations of the *T.K.* we liked it.

We started out again early on Tuesday morning. Hearing of a twenty-four hour opening in the Georgia Strait, we dipped our nets, mostly to work out any twists, and caught nothing but a few dogfish. Moving on, we reached Sabine Channel by mid-afternoon and set out our nets again. A passing cash buyer said the average catch farther up the Channel was forty sockeye, so we let the net drift for an hour with high expectations. Valerie and I put on our aprons and gloves, ready to start picking fish, but when I tried to start the engine to run the drum drive, there was only a high-pitched whine. The starter shaft had broken.

I hauled the net in by hand, seldom interrupted by salmon caught in it. By the time I was done, the wind had stiffened. Leaving the end of the net out to act as a drogue to keep the stern into the waves and soften our ride, I tried to raise Otto on the Mickey Mouse. There was no reply, despite repeated calls. The rocky shore of Texada Island was drawing closer. I had thrown emergency flares and a few other things into a bag and had a line ready. If the *T.K.* was going to hit the beach, our plan was to leap ashore at the last second. The line would keep us from getting separated.

We were oddly calm waiting for the impact when Otto arrived. He swung around in a tight circle and came up alongside the *T.K.* What likely saved us was that he hadn't stowed the towing line he'd used on Sunday and had it ready. He threw it to me like a rodeo cowboy while his boat was still moving. I snubbed it around our bow cleat as he ran back to his wheelhouse. Smoke belched from his stack as he shifted the Bolinder into full forward. The towing line snapped tight, nearly shearing the cleat off our deck. A lucky grab at the mast guywire kept me from flying overboard as the *T.K.* was swung clear of the rocks, just as I thought I heard them tickle its hull.

With nowhere close for shelter on that side of Texada, Otto towed us toward Lasqueti Island. Our relief at escaping the rocks was so great we hardly noticed the *T.K.*'s wild rolling as we crossed the Sabine Channel. There was a sheltered spot between Boho and Lasqueti Islands that Otto knew about. He dropped anchor there and we rafted up beside his boat.

"My gootness, vhat excitement!" he exclaimed as we sat down at his galley table. His eyes were still so wide that the whites showed all around his irises.

"Vhy you not call me on Meeky Mouse?" he asked, pouring us tea and putting out his stale cookies, butter, and delicious honey.

"I did," I told him. "Maybe you were picking your net and didn't hear me."

"Yah, maybe. I had big catch. Dogfish, sonamagun," he laughed.

I knew him well enough by then to tell if he was annoyed by all the delays to the trip caused by our breakdowns. His moods were always plain on his face. Oddly, he seemed to be enjoying himself. When I tried to thank him for all his help, he wouldn't hear any of it. That night when we were in bed, Valerie told me she thought he had been dreadfully lonely and we were in some way filling some of the void left by the family that he'd lost.

Wednesday dawned with the wind still blowing. We had decided around Otto's table the night before that our best chance to get the *T.K.* repaired was to tow it across Malaspina Strait to Pender Harbour. The sea had to be relatively calm for that, but it was far from calm from what we could see looking out over Sabine Channel. The storm didn't blow itself out until the evening, forcing us to stay put, but the day wasn't uneventful.

First we heard the jingling of bells and looked out to see a herd of feral goats looking at us from the beach on Lasqueti Island. They were more skittish and unruly than farm goats. A couple of them waded into the water as if to swim out and have a closer look at us, but then something alarmed them and they scrambled up the bank and disappeared. One of the collectors working that area later told us the goats were escapees from the hippie farm communes on Lasqueti.

As the tide dropped during the day, a huge rock rose up from the water behind us. From the look of it, the keel of Otto's boat had just cleared it on the way into the anchorage. It was blanketed in starfish, prompting Valerie and me to get our skiff down and row over to look at them. On our way back we noticed a rock shelf on the Boho Island shore filled with oysters. We filled up the bottom of the skiff for our dinner. When Otto saw us opening them, he made a face and said he couldn't understand how people could eat those things. Valerie gave him one for a taste as she started to fry them, and insisted he try it. He did so, under protest, and then we heard: "My gootness. My gootness, vhat delicatess!"

He ended up eating more than Valerie or me.

On Thursday morning, the sea was calm and we got underway at 4:30 a.m., arriving in Pender Harbour at 9:00 a.m. I took the starter out of the engine and caught a Tyee Airways flight into Vancouver with it at 11:30 and was back with a new one on the evening flight. By midnight, it was installed and we were asleep.

Apart from the engine troubles, our trip so far had been a cruise through a paradise of calm green waters, cedar-lined shores, and some interesting houses with lawns that ran down to the sea. Our first stop after leaving Pender

Harbour on Friday morning was Stuart Island, where we fuelled up. Leaving the dock at Stuart Island, a few of the skippers tied up there had given us an odd look. I put it down to the *T.K.* and the *Joker Too* being such an odd couple. It didn't occur to me that their looks might have something to do with what was ahead.

My freshly bought charts were on the wheelhouse dashboard. They had to be folded over because the space was so cramped, but I'd kept an eye on them as we went along. I'd noticed that the Yuculta Rapids were up ahead. Otto and some of the other gillnetters I'd met called them the "Yuka-toss" and said they could be big trouble if entered at the wrong time. All I knew was that we were in a passage named Calm Channel; the waters up ahead didn't look all that different from those we'd seen on the way up, and I'd been through fast-flowing rapids on much smaller boats than the *T.K.*

Twenty minutes out from the Stuart Island dock, the *Joker Too*, running a couple of boat's lengths ahead of us, was abruptly flung to one side as if it were no more than a wood chip on the water. Seconds later, we went shooting after it like a torpedo, just grazing its stern rollers as we swept past. There was no controlling the *T.K.*, and it was plain to see Otto was having the same trouble. The water had begun to boil around us. Just as quickly as our boats had almost smashed into each other, they were flung apart again. The steering wheel was nearly useless as the current caught us, but I gradually coaxed the boat nearer the shore where the water was smoother. Otto was now a hundred yards ahead of us. We followed him through a narrow passage, so close to the black rocks of the shore that we could smell the seaweed on them. We came out into a wider channel, and the water seemed calm again. Valerie and I looked at each other and began to relax a little.

Glancing at the chart for our location, words and symbols I hadn't noticed before leapt out at me: DEVIL'S HOLE. Printed in violet beside its name was the note: CAUTION: VIOLENT EDDIES AND WHIRLPOOLS FORM IN DEVIL'S HOLE. The symbols were three small helixes in the stretch of water between Devil's Hole and Dent Rapids. This was where we were heading.

By now over-falls were forming on the surface ahead of us, slowly undulating like giant snakes. We hit them seconds later. The boat was spun sideways and listed sharply. We slowed to a crawl. A low roar like that of a waterfall came up. Through it, somehow, I could hear the boat's tiller chains snapping and sliding in their chases as the rudder was buffeted by the current. I hadn't checked them before leaving Vancouver and prayed they'd hold up. If they broke, there would be no saving us.

Another surprise waited ahead: a giant whirlpool with a cloud of vapour rising from the middle of it. As we got closer, we could hear a sort of rushing noise over the sound of the engine. We could feel the whirlpool begin to take us, and the boat listed toward its centre. Looking down into it, we could see a fully grown alder tree, its roots washed clean, swirling in the vortex. Out of instinct, or more likely sheer terror, I cranked the wheel away and gunned the engine into full throttle. Hesitantly, the bow began to turn toward safety. The boat pivoted on the rim of the whirlpool and the stern swung over the vortex. Breaking out of the water, the propeller made the engine scream for a few seconds until it bit in again as the boat swung around. It gave us the kick we needed to break free and make for calmer water near the shore.

I edged the *T.K.* as close as I dared toward the boulders lining the water, not caring if the hull scraped them, trying to get as far away from the whirlpool as I could. Little wavelets lapped over the sand among the boulders as if reassuring us we were safe. I slipped the boat out of gear and put my arms around Valerie for a long hug. I might have needed it more than she did.

"Don't ever do that again," she said, not a waver in her voice.

I didn't answer, not sure my voice would be as steady.

Otto had anchored in a cove a mile up the channel to wait for us. He had passed through the area where the whirlpool had appeared without much more than a few cross currents, and was astonished by our story. He insisted on making tea and staying anchored where we were for a while so we could recover from the ordeal. Otto was not an easy man to convince otherwise once he'd made up his mind, so I rafted the *T.K.* securely to the *Joker Too* and switched off the engine. The silence hit us like a shock after the uproar of the previous few hours and we sat on Otto's hatch cover soaking it up. We idled away a few hours that way. At one point, I broke out the fishing tackle. He and Valerie each caught a good-sized rock cod, which we later cooked for our supper. I checked the boat for damage after our wild ride and found the usual heavy leakage from the garboard planks. We started off again late in the day and anchored for the night in Forward Harbour.

We were off not long after dawn the next day and stopped for fuel in Sointula. I noticed the odd-looking barns in the fields around the village as we approached the fuel dock. After fuelling up, I asked Otto about them. As usual, he had a story. In his version, a religious zealot from Finland founded the village. A self-described atheist, Otto was usually dismissive of preachers, but not in this case. He seemed to find this one amusing because, as he told it, the flock was all women. They had come with the preacher from Finland around the turn of the twentieth century looking for a place to set up a new utopia. They settled on Malcolm Island and set to work clearing the land and building barns like the ones I had seen.

The flaw in the preacher's plan was that many of the women had left men behind in Finland. When it dawned on them that their women might not be coming back, the men headed for Sointula to round them up. Some liked what they saw and stayed. What became of the preacher wasn't clear, but Otto thought he may have been done in by one of the newly arrived men.

True to Otto's version of their heritage, many of the men and women we saw in the village were blond and blue-eyed and spoke Finnish among themselves. Otto could speak their language, and our departure kept getting delayed while he visited with people who seemed to be long-lost friends. There were several stout, good-looking women, whose company we saw Otto enjoying later in the day. Valerie and I ended up spending the night tied up at a small dock a little way from the fuel barge, quite happily left alone without a sign of Otto.

The next morning we had a late start. An apologetic, red-eyed Otto led the way. He set a course straight as an arrow down the middle of the channel, which I suspected was controlled by his autopilot while he dozed in his heated helm seat. I kept track of our progress on my charts for future reference. Just past Hardy Bay, as we were entering Goletas Channel, Otto surprised us. He abruptly veered to port and appeared to head straight toward the rocky shoreline. I called him on the Mickey Mouse, but there was no answer. Thinking he'd fallen asleep, I cranked up our speed to overtake him. I was weighing my chances of jumping aboard like a movie cowboy onto a stagecoach as we drew even with the *Joker Too*. Then I noticed an opening in the rock wall at the shoreline. As we neared it, a gillnetter appeared out of the opening as if by magic, and sailed off in the direction of Port Hardy. It had to be the entrance to the Duval Point fish camp we'd heard so much about. Seeing that Otto was in full control, we dropped back to follow him again. He slowed down and led us into the opening. Surprisingly, it turned out to be wide enough for two boats to pass each other with comfortable clearance.

Entering the camp for the first time, after all we'd been through to get there, I had an inkling of how it must have felt for explorers entering a forbidden city—except the fish camp was no city. The largest thing there was a scow, which must have been squeezed through the opening between the rocks at high tide. It was anchored near the entrance to the camp, as if guarding it. On its deck were two buildings, a large two-storey corrugated metal structure and a smaller one, along with fuel tanks and net racks. A large, old vessel, which I took to be a packer, was tied up alongside. Rafted up to it were several smaller boats, which I knew were collectors from having seen them in Georgia Strait when fishing the previous fall. Long floating docks were connected to the scow and led off into a wide lagoon ringed by a sandy beach. Gillnetters, some rafted together three and four deep, were moored all along both sides of these docks.

Throttling back to dead slow, we followed Otto along the outside dock until he found an open spot at the end. People along the dock and aboard the boats tied up to it stopped what they were doing to watch our progress. Several of the boats with larger decks had tarps over their booms rigged as awnings. It was cloudy and cool, but men were seated under them around makeshift tables that held wine bottles and plates of food in a way that reminded me of Italy. That may also have been from the way they craned their necks to get a better look at my deckhand as we went past.

Not to detract from Valerie, who turned everyone's head when they first saw her, but the highlight of their day may have been my attempt at mooring the *T.K.* The tide was running, and when I tried to turn on a dime as Otto had done ahead of us, my dime kept slipping away from the dock and

I made a hash of it. Finally, one of the men who had been talking to Otto came over, caught the line I threw him, and quickly tied it to a cleat. Leaving me to pull the *T.K.* in the rest of the way, he went and talked to Otto again. It was hard to tell if he was rude, shy, or merely disgusted with my boat handling. Otto introduced him as Matt, an old friend, but we weren't invited into their conversation. That suited us because we wanted to go exploring.

The camp wasn't large compared to ones we fished from later, but it was a new world for us, and fascinating. Francis Millerd and Sons, a fishing company that had been around for generations, ran the camp. The heart of it was the scow. There was a general store, laundry, and showers in the large building on its deck. Company offices and staff quarters were upstairs. A radio aerial flying the company flag on its guy wires was mounted on top of the large building. The ice plant, with its generators and compressors going around the clock, was in the small building. Each of the gillnetters tied up along the docks flew the same flag, blue-and-white quarters diagonally opposed. Otto, who delivered fish to several fishing companies and had a supply of their different flags, had given us one to fly off our rigging before entering the camp.

In the office, we got our "book fish" from the company. This was for recording our catch numbers and species upon delivery to the company collectors, and it was the basis on which we were paid out, either on request during the season or at the end of the year. The book also let us shop in the store on credit, provided we had enough deliveries showing, and gave us shower and laundry privileges.

One of our first surprises as we explored was the number of women on the docks. There were some who looked at home in the camp, as if they'd come back year after year as deckhands for their mates. They were mostly dressed in jeans and doeskin shirts with not a flash of lipstick or nail polish among them. These women were middle-aged, no-nonsense types who looked like they could handle a gillnetter on their own with no trouble. They sized us up with direct looks as we passed them.

"Maybe you'll grow up to be just like them," I said to Valerie out of the side of my mouth. She punched me in the shoulder, and some of the women smiled.

On the dock farthest from the entrance to the lagoon, we ran into women of a different type: hippies in full regalia. They were sitting around in front of boats painted in strange colours and hung with macramé curtains. The nets on their drums looked like rags and the boats exuded incense and decrepitude. The only sign of industry was a bearded man with a ponytail who was knotting hanging twine into fancy shapes. His fingers were long and slender, not the type to be ripping salmon out of a gillnet. Although the week's fishery was due to open in a few hours, there was no sign of preparations being made on any of the boats tied up there.

In contrast to the hippie vessels, there was a sense of urgency on all the other boats we passed on our way back to the *T.K.* A few had already left the camp to stake out their favourite spot, and others were lined up waiting for fuel alongside the scow. Packers were moored along the sides of the scow ready to receive fish, either directly from collectors who had unloaded gillnetters on the fishing grounds, or from the gillnetters themselves when they came into camp. The packers were mostly large old vessels, some over eighty feet long. Their crews were busy loading ice into their vessels by chutes from the ice plant on the scow in preparation for the first deliveries the following morning. Once loaded, these packers would run the fish into Vancouver for processing, then make a quick return trip to camp, often carrying supplies for the general store.

We ran into Matt again on our way back to the *T.K.* He was much friendlier this time and stopped to talk. A tall, white-haired man with a strong Croatian accent, he joked a lot and struck us as Otto's opposite right from the start. Matt didn't seem affected by the increasing excitement in the air as the six o'clock opening drew near. We didn't know if he was serious when he said he was going to eat supper before going out and he still had to cook it. He was planning a clam risotto from clams he'd picked from the shore of the lagoon, a cauliflower salad, and a green salad, washed down with his homemade red wine. Valerie couldn't help asking how he made the risotto and how he dressed the cauliflower salad. It struck a nerve and they had a ten-minute conversation about cooking, oblivious to all the boats leaving the docks around us to go fishing.

Matt was still tied up when we followed Otto out into Goletas Channel soon after to chase down our first sockeye in northern waters. There was a smell of something delicious coming out Matt's galley window as we passed.

The weather held throughout the four days of the opening, and we found the fishing better than it had been off Vancouver. Although the winds came up in the afternoon, we found spots around the Gordon Islands that were relatively sheltered, and discovered the fishing was better at night. We caught our first two smileys (spring salmon or Chinooks), weighing around thirty pounds each during that opening. Springs were called smileys because they meant big money, especially the red springs, which could sell for over three dollars a pound. They always brought a smile to a skipper's face as they came up over the rollers.

When the fishery closed the following Thursday, we heard that Matt's was one of the high boats. Needless to say, we did nowhere near as well, but as Valerie pointed out, at least a tugboat hadn't wrecked our net.

I had a chance to ask Matt how he did it when he invited us to his boat for a glass of wine after the closing.

"Fish the tides," he'd said. "Watch me next time; I show you."

When I told Otto about this, he said, "Ahh, fishing tides is big baloney. You vatch me. I show you how bedder to fish."

It began to dawn on us that we'd have to do some delicate manoeuvring in later openings to avoid offending either of our teachers. I started to pay close attention to the tide tables and did find the best fishing on slack water. When the tide was running, we didn't catch as much. We'd notice Matt slipping back into camp for a quick nap during those times, but we stayed out with our net in the water to keep Otto company.

The weather was good on our weekends in camp. We saw Otto and Matt for morning coffee every day. Afterwards, Otto would go off to repair some new thing on his boat and Matt joined his friends on the boats with tarps over their decks. They laughed and talked well into the evening when coils of smoking insect repellent were put out against the invasion of mosquitoes. Throughout the day, music played on different parts of the docks, there were bursts of laughter, the smells of steaks and salmon being barbecued were everywhere, and people were out sunbathing on the decks of their boats. On Fridays, Valerie and I would row our skiff to the beach and collect clams. We'd give some to Matt, and the rest Valerie turned into clam chowder later that weekend. It was the best I'd ever tasted. We ate it with chunks of surprisingly fresh Italian bread from the general store and a bottle of Matt's red wine. We'd linger over the meal well into the evening.

"So this is fishing," I said to Valerie on one of those nights. "If only we'd known earlier."

I may have spoken too soon.

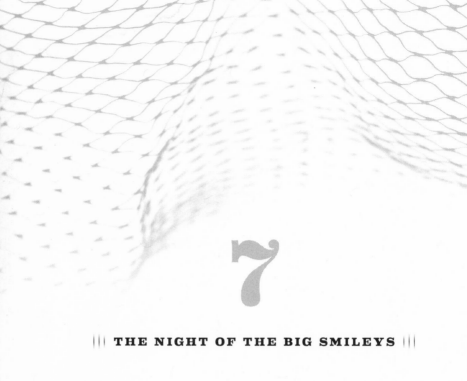

7

||| THE NIGHT OF THE BIG SMILEYS |||

The Friday afternoon of our third full weekend in the camp, the last one before Valerie had to fly back to Vancouver for work, we rowed our skiff out to the beach at low tide and collected a couple of buckets of clams as usual. One of our new friends had shown us how to put oatmeal in the clams to clean out their sand and grit, and we left them out on our deck for Sunday morning when Valerie planned to make chowder to take out with us for the next opening at six o'clock that afternoon.

On Saturday, we slept in until mid-morning, then made a run into Port Hardy to make arrangements for Valerie's flight back to Vancouver. We did some shopping for chowder ingredients and stopped for burgers and fries in a café near the fish docks. While eating, we read a day-old *Vancouver Province* from cover to cover and were back in camp by four in the afternoon with our appetites for greasy fries sated. At dusk we went for a walk on the docks before going to bed and saw a cougar prowling the shore just above the clam bed where we had been digging the day before. He moved along unhurriedly, his long tawny form reflected perfectly in the shiny green water of the bay. We watched him until he vanished in the shadows of the cedars. Sunday morning after breakfast we looked for the spot where we had seen him, but the tide was up and there was only a thin line of sand between the water and the foot of the cedar forest.

Afterwards, Valerie made her chowder and we invited Otto for lunch. He became more restless by the minute as he sat on our hatch cover waiting for the chowder to be served. Finishing long before us, he abruptly stood up and bolted back to his boat with barely a goodbye. It was a state Otto always seemed to get into before an opening, although this time he seemed a little worse than normal. Valerie and I took a quick walk around the docks to stretch our legs and by the time we were back, he had his engine running and was about to cast off. Otto said he'd be heading for the spot he'd told us about near the Gordon Group islands where he'd had some good sets. He wanted to get there early to make sure no one else took it. It was only three o'clock, which meant he'd be jogging in that spot for two hours or so to protect it. That wasn't for us. We helped him cast off and said we'd look for him when we got out, but it wouldn't be until much closer to six, the official opening time.

After we saw Otto off, Valerie and I walked over to have a look for Matt. As on other afternoons before the fishery opened, there were no signs of preparation on his boat. The net cover was still on his drum and his hatch covers were stacked the way he'd left them to dry out the fish holds when he'd washed them down after the previous week's fishing. He was inside cooking his dinner, having a glass of wine, and invited us in. Valerie and Matt had a long discussion about what he was cooking before he finally got around to talking about fishing. He told us that there was a gale blowing in from the Pacific, straight through the Goletas Channel. It wouldn't die down until at least midnight, but it would be too foul for any kind of fishing until morning. As if to emphasize what he was saying, we noticed the water in the lagoon rising and falling slightly, despite the sheltering rocks that protected it from the Goletas Channel.

After leaving Matt and talking it over, we decided to stick our nose out of the lagoon to see what the weather was really like before deciding to lose a night's fishing. If it was as bad as Matt predicted, we'd turn around and head back into camp and not try to venture out again until morning. Otherwise, we'd find our way over to the sheltered area where Otto was fishing and stay out.

The entrance to the lagoon was protected from the northwest by a barren island of humped rock. As we cleared it, the wind, howling like a jet plane, threw us sideways and the waves hit our little, narrow-gutted boat broadside, nearly rolling us over. The clam chowder and the hot coffee, just made for the evening's fishing, flew out of their clamps on the stove and spattered everywhere, leaving the empty pots skittering around the trunk cabin floor. Our big jar of home-made granola flew out of the locker and joined them. Spray flying off the bow raked the wheelhouse windows. I could barely see where we were going. Despite the weather, there must have been a hundred boats in the channel just then, all starting to set their nets. Getting turned around in that sea among those boats would have been unwise to say the least. All I could do was keep going.

Finally we got through the fleet and reached a spot where I could have turned around more or less safely. By then we had become used to the conditions and it made sense to try setting our net before heading back to camp. I left the wheel to Valerie and went to see what I could do. Most of the other boats already had their nets out by then. I started our set fairly close to one of the boats, but the wind was so strong that we were well clear by the time I'd finished setting. Once the net was out, it kept our stern into the sea, changing the boat's ride from frantic twisting rolls to moderate bucking as it crested each wave. This was more tolerable, and we were able to have a look around to see where we'd ended up. Everything was unfamiliar. None of the land masses were recognizable, nor were any of the boats around us. In all the excitement, I had forgotten about looking for Otto, and he was nowhere in sight.

We picked our set after an hour and had a dozen sockeye. By then the wind was blowing harder and the waves stood taller than me. Setting across the wind would have been impossible with the way the boat rolled, so we merely set out downwind and held on. As it got dark, the weather grew worse and the other boats began to disappear. We thought about heading back to camp, but it would have meant running in a beam sea, which the *T.K.* had already shown us it didn't like. Besides, I didn't think I could find the narrow entrance to the camp in the dark. Our best chance, maybe our only chance, was to ride out the weather and stay put.

By midnight, waves were smashing over our stern rollers. The scuppers were overwhelmed and the cockpit was awash. I had the deck bucket handy to start bailing if it got any worse. We'd already survived one scare. The boat had been bucking so violently that the cork line had jumped the net rollers and slid sideways along the rail. As the line slacked off, the boat had sheared. Cresting another wave, the line had snapped tight again. This kicked the boat around again with such force it could have easily torn the drum stand out from the cockpit and capsized us. Sliding around in the heaving cockpit, we managed to wrestle the cork line back inside the rollers and lash it in place. That kept the boat on a line with the net, which was acting as a drogue to keep us stern-to into the waves. It was our only chance of surviving that sea.

By this time the lights of Port Hardy, which had been visible far off to starboard for the past hour, had disappeared. We'd lost the Deserters Group light, and only the Masterman Island light could still be seen to give us some sort of bearing. We were miles from where we'd made our set in territory we had only seen at a distance on the last leg of our run up from Vancouver. All I could remember of it was a rocky shoreline and foaming reefs a mile or two from our port side, and the width and blue-grey emptiness of Queen Charlotte Sound to starboard. This time we were heading the other way; the shoreline and reefs were to starboard, distance unknown, and the sea was a roaring, terrifying blackness.

Wedged in beside the drum to counter the boat's heaving, I regretted not taking Matt's advice to wait in camp until the storm blew itself out. He was probably sleeping peacefully in his bunk while we were going through this hell. The *T.K.*, after fifty or so years of hard use, was leaking badly. The garboard seams were leaking even worse than on my first night of gillnetting with Blake. The electric bilge pumps were running so often that I had to keep the engine going just to keep the batteries charged enough to feed them. They wouldn't have been able to keep up but for the manual deck pump. Earlier that night, we were pumping ten strokes every hour before sucking air. Now we were pumping ten strokes every fifteen minutes and still not getting all the water out. If anything was to happen to that pump—and it was only a flimsy rig built of galvanized sheet metal—it was unlikely we could have made it to the closest shore before sinking, even if the electric pumps kept working.

We were all by ourselves now. The light of the last boat in sight had disappeared well before midnight. There might have been a few desperadoes still out somewhere, but not close enough that we could see their lights. Radar would have been handy to pick them out and to tell us how far away that starboard shore with the foaming reefs was, but in those days radar wasn't common and it was well beyond our budget anyway. We might have tried to raise somebody on the radio, but our Mickey Mouse only had a range of a mile or two at best. New radios, along with a depth sounder and a decent compass, were first on our shopping list once fishing started to pay off—assuming we were alive to collect the earnings.

What really worried me was the engine. The Gray Marine was hard to start and had a tendency to flood and leak gas until it got going. Its worst feature was the external shaft to the water pump, which connected through two rubber discs that acted as universal joints. Once the engine got hot, the discs warmed up and stretched a bit, sometimes letting go of the connecting shaft. This had happened several times when we were fall fishing. When the shaft and discs dropped into the bilge, the water pump stopped working and the engine quickly overheated. As there was no temperature alarm on the engine, our only warning was from a gauge that was a little stiff. By the time its needle started to move out of the normal operating range, the engine was already boiling hot and had to be shut down immediately to avoid cracking the block.

When the shaft and discs dropped out, they had to be retrieved by reaching down beside the hot engine and groping around in the muck of the bilge. Once it took me a minute to find everything, but another time it took fifteen. It wasn't hard to reconnect the shaft once the parts were recovered. The hard part was waiting, dead in the water, for the engine to cool down, and then starting it without blowing up the boat since that was when the carburetor usually leaked gas. The times I'd had to deal with it had been in daylight and calm water, and it was frightening even then. The possibility of engine trouble that night was something I refused to think about.

Taking over the deck pump to give Valerie a break, I kept an eye on the water level in the cockpit, the light at the end of our net, which was miraculously still burning, and the Masterman Island light, which appeared to be getting fainter in the distance. All the while I was watching out in every direction for the terror of all night-fishing gillnetters: widely spaced navigation lights approaching out of the darkness, showing both red and green. That meant a freighter or big tug was bearing down on us, oblivious to our existence and about to end it.

I felt the wind drop, or thought I did, so I groped my way into the wheelhouse to see if Valerie felt it. She wasn't sure, but thought she had. Wary of false hopes, she didn't want to say anything until she was sure. I stayed with her for a bit, but there was too much noise from the storm to talk much, and we were both still tense from the wild ride we'd been on. I went back out to the pump a few minutes later.

Now the wind definitely seemed lighter, and the noise of the sea might have diminished a bit. It still took ten strokes of the pump to clear the bilge, but the water swirling around under the drum wasn't as deep. For the first time that night, I began to think we'd make it through.

It was time to pick the net again, and we started off hoping to continue the trend of the night. The first set had brought in a dozen sockeye. From the second we picked thirty, as well as two big smileys. Our work light was reassuring against the pounding waves as we peered over the rollers to see what the net would bring in. The water was a luminescent green under the light; in a way we found it captivating and beautiful, no matter the weather, and it was no different this time.

As the cork line wound onto the drum and the end of the net came closer, the stern of the *T.K.* began to lose its buoyancy. It plunged deeper into the troughs as we slid down the backs of the waves, each time throwing sheets of green water over the rollers. The net was coming in slowly, and I had to rev the engine to keep it from stalling. There was something heavy in the net, most likely a log, but we knew from the musky odour rising that there had to be a smiley involved as well. It was a smell we had memorized and hoped for every set. Timing my move between waves, I looked over the rollers and saw a tangled mess hanging straight down into the depths. It wasn't a log dragging down the net, it was a bundle of fish, sockeye from the look of them, with at least two smileys showing. Now the storm didn't matter at all as we anticipated the sound of more smileys thumping down at our feet.

The weight of the net was beyond the power of our engine to handle, and the boat was bucking around so much we couldn't get braced enough to help the drum pull it up. Finally realizing the sea might help us, I let out some of the net and, as the stern dipped into another trough, we heaved, timing our pull with the uplift of the next wave. The bundle came aboard so suddenly we both fell back against the drum under a tangle of net and fish. Pulling apart the mess, we found ten sockeye and three smileys, all in the thirty-pound range. The remainder of the set brought in another forty sockeye, and yet another large smiley.

As we set out the net again, we found for the first time that night we could talk to each other without shouting. We also found we were ravenous. Between spelling me off at the pump, and keeping an eye on the engine temperature gauge, Valerie had managed to clean up the mess in the trunk cabin. She had also put on a fresh pot of coffee just before starting to help me re-set our net. The coffee was now ready, and its aroma chased out the last of our fears about the storm. The wind was dying down further, and the rain had become a drizzle. It was still too cold and wet to have our coffee sitting on the hatch cover, as we normally did while drifting on a set, so we drank it standing up in the wheelhouse instead. It was now nearly eleven hours since we'd had anything to eat. The store-bought cookies we had with the coffee were starting to taste like the most delicious thing we had ever eaten.

Our earlier fears were replaced with confidence and pride for toughing out the worst storm we'd ever been in. Looking back, the Yuculta Rapids and Devil's Hole seemed like amusement park rides in comparison. What's more, we had fish to show for our efforts. In fact, we had already caught twice as many as we had on our previous best day's fishing.

Dawn was still a couple of hours away, and anything could happen, but we knew we'd won. In our relief, we couldn't stop talking and laughing at the slightest sign of wit from either of us. Six strokes every half hour were all it took to empty the bilge now. The engine temperature gauge hadn't budged all night. Even if the connecting shaft and discs were to drop into the bilge, I knew I could find them and get the engine running again without much trouble.

It came as a shock at first to see light coming down from the heavens, but then we realized that the clouds were thinning and a nearly full moon was shining. For the rest of the night, it was our company, sometimes partly hidden by scudding clouds and sometimes fully exposed, but always drawing our eyes to itself.

Our coffee break turned into a full meal when we realized how hungry we were. On the menu were hard-boiled eggs, fried Argentinian corned beef, a large can of pork and beans, hard tack with cheddar cheese and thick slices of Spanish onion, and canned peaches for dessert. After a meal like that, nothing in the world could have defeated us.

Once we were finished eating, we picked the net again, this time in silvery moonlight with a moderate chop, and the wind backed off to a stiff breeze. Before starting, we noticed the cork line was down quite deep in four or five places. Things looked good for more smileys, we told ourselves with our newfound optimism, as we began to pull in the net. There have been many nights since that one when I've looked at a net with the corks down in the same way and expected smileys, only to find dogfish or deadheads—but not this time. Once again, that distinctive musky smell came to us well before the fish arrived, and each time they were big ones, five in all, including one black monster that looked close to fifty pounds. Along with the smileys were another forty sockeye and two coho.

We re-set the net downwind again, going with our luck, although the sea had calmed to such an extent that setting across the wind would have been just as easy. There was a new heaviness to the boat now. For a moment I thought we'd sprung a monstrous leak, but a few strokes of the deck pump showed nothing different in the bilge. The *T.K.* was merely reacting to the weight of the fish in its holds. We added to it by another forty sockeye and three smileys when we picked that set.

It was nearly full daylight by the time we made our dawn set; the wind had died and the sea was down to a light chop. The lights of Port Hardy, which we had swept past earlier in the night, re-appeared just before dawn. My guess was that we were eight miles or so off Masterman Island, which put us an hour and a half away from the camp. By the time we finished picking the dawn set, we had over two hundred sockeye, sixteen smileys, six coho, a few jack springs, and a couple of rockfish. It was the best one-night catch we ever had on that old boat, and by far our best night for smileys ever. The holds were full and there were twenty sockeye sliding around under the drum from the last set. If we had tried, we might have added to the stories about catches so great that the bunks were filled with fish, but the dawn breeze was turning into a stiff wind and the sea looked ready to rise again. Fully remembering what that could lead to, we began the trek back to the fish camp.

By the time we were halfway across the mouth of Hardy Bay, we saw boats coming toward us from around Duval Point. One was leading, another half dozen fanned out behind. As they came closer, we recognized Matt's boat in the lead with the *Joker Too* among the following boats. We cut our speed until we were jogging into the waves to keep head-way. The sea had already risen a good deal since we'd picked the dawn set, but the added weight had made the *T.K.* more stable and ready to punch through waves with authority.

When Matt came up to us he thrust his head and shoulders out of his wheelhouse window and looked at us as if we'd come back from the dead.

"Holy momma!" he shouted. "You guys okay? I no sleep all night for worry! We come look for boat wreck. We think you dead for sure!"

"He's only kidding, isn't he?" Valerie said.

"Yeah, you know what a kidder he is," I replied.

Otto and the other skippers we'd gotten to know from our weeks in the camp pulled up around Matt.

"What's the matter with your boat?" one of them shouted. "You sinking or did you load up?"

"We loaded up," I shouted back, with a strange tight-ness in my throat. Realizing that these men had come out to search for us had affected me.

"Good show!" the man shouted and laughed. A couple of them sounded their whistles, and then they were gone to start their week's fishing.

One of them must have radioed ahead to the camp, because when we arrived at the scow to deliver our catch, the scow manager was there to shake our hands and admire the fish. He said he'd never seen that many smileys delivered from a night's fishing.

After treating ourselves to a few hours' sleep tied up at the dock, our net was down again on the next slack tide that afternoon. It was another good catch, adding to the evidence that fishing the tides worked better than throwing out the net at random. When the tide turned, we were close enough to camp to run in for another couple of hours' sleep before going out again. Matt was already there.

Our catches for the rest of that week's fishing didn't come close to that first night's, but they were respectable. The company was paying seventy cents a pound for sockeye in those days and the sockeye we were catching weighed an average of just under six pounds each. Counting that first night's catch, we made over four thousand dollars on the week, more than double what the *T.K.* had cost. As we relaxed after making our last delivery, our talk drifted to what kind of boat we'd look for after the season was done, and maybe even building a new one a little further down the line. It didn't need saying that in four days' fishing we'd earned almost twice as much as I made in a month as an architect.

Otto wanted to know all about how we had managed to survive that savage first night. He said he'd looked for us and thought we had decided to stay in camp until morning. Even with his heavy boat, the weather was so bad he had pulled in his net and gone for shelter among the Gordon Group islands. When I told him that one of the reasons we had stayed out was because I didn't think I could find the entrance to the camp in the dark, he gave me an instant lesson in nighttime coastal navigation.

"Always keep eye on skyline," he said. "Even vhen blowink and sky black, land more black. Alvays you find sometink on skyline to line up vhere you vant to go. Vork like gun sight."

On the coast, the horizon was usually a mountain range, and prominent ridges or notches along its top could be used as a sighting line for entrances such as the one into the fish camp. This worked at night because the mountains were always blacker than the sky, no matter how dark it was, just as Otto had said. It was a simple trick, and I've used it up and down the coast many times since, each time remembering Otto.

Otto seemed a little put out that we hadn't found him and fished nearby this time. He seemed to sense we had adopted some of Matt's approach to fishing, even though he had labelled it "big baloney." He seemed sad rather than angry. Although Otto didn't have the words to express himself, we were touched, and made an effort to do things with him on the weekend. That was probably why, when he talked about going to a spot he knew about to can fish, we agreed to go along.

The spot he was talking about turned out to be across the Goletas Channel on the far side of Nigei Island, as I discovered by tracking our route on my charts. It was nearly a two-hour trip. The last leg of the trip was through a narrow, twisting channel into a lagoon that wasn't much wider than the one around our fish camp.

There was something about the place, the smell or the stillness or the darkness emanating from the surrounding cedars that made Valerie uneasy, even as we were anchoring. I soon caught what she was feeling. The odour was oddly sulphurous. The edge of the cedar forest along the water was impenetrable and mysterious, not at all like the one at our camp. It was a dead silence—no sound of birds, not even crows. We must have looked like we needed reassuring, because Otto tried to calm our unease, telling us how sunny and peaceful it was when he'd canned fish there the year before.

It was late by then, and we got ready for bed early so we could get up and get our canning done the next day. I had instinctively taken to doing a final check of the boat before going to sleep, even when rafted up beside Otto, as we were then. Besides, after learning about the importance of tides from Matt, I was trying to keep track of them wherever we were. When I checked the tables standing in the wheelhouse that night, they showed a zero tide. Curious about what that could mean for us, I turned on the spotlight and swept it over the lagoon. It showed a forest of old wooden pilings, their ends rotted into sharp points emerging all around our boats. It didn't take much of an imagination to see one of them punching through our hull as the tide ebbed. The strange smell intensified and the eerie silence was so strong I heard it over the blood rushing in my ears.

"Otto, are you up?" I yelled. "Have a look at this."

"Yaw, yaw, I comink," he shouted back. "Somet'ing wake me up already!"

Valerie, hearing the shouting, came up to the wheel-house, already in her jeans and pulling on a sweater. She stared at the sight around us. "My God, what's all that?"

"Old pilings from buildings that used to be here, I think. I read that toredos ate the tops away into points like that."

"What if we're on top of one?"

"Bad news, but we would already have found out," I said, trying to sound reassuring.

"How fast can we get out of here?"

By the time I got my engine started, Otto already had his going and was pulling in his anchor. Valerie and I untied the lines holding our two boats together and I followed close behind the Joker Too, threading the pilings toward the chan-nel that had led us into the lagoon. It was a run through a night blacker than any I had ever seen. Our spotlights could barely penetrate the murk. The tide was so low that our keels scraped bottom and more than once we came almost to a standstill. Low-growing tree limbs we hadn't noticed on the way in clawed at our boats. Much of the lagoon had drained into mud flats stretching up to the cedars. The very centre of it was just deep enough for our boats to get through, and I could see mud and bottom debris churning up in Otto's wake.

They say the way out of somewhere always seems shorter than the way in. It was the opposite in that channel. Each time it seemed we'd sprung free, another branch scraped our boats and more of the bottom mud was kicked up in Otto's wake. Finally, after a half dozen false hopes of breaking free, we felt the dead water of the channel rising and falling, as if coming back to life. Wavelets began to form and a sea breeze sweetened the air. A few minutes later we had crossed the surf line and were riding the swells in Queen Charlotte Strait. Otto threw us a line and we pulled the *T.K.* close enough to shout and joke back and forth. We were so giddy we laughed at everything.

"You know," Otto shouted, "I so scairt piles be coming up arse of *Joker Too*—sorry, Valerie—I not sit down myself on whole way out!" It was so unexpected, coming from Otto, that it brought the biggest laugh.

Rather than going back to the camp, we decided to tie up for what was left of the night in a tiny cove some people called God's Pocket, just a short run down Christie Pass from where we celebrated our breakout. It was where skippers wanting to cross Queen Charlotte Sound traditionally tied up for the night so they could make an early start in the morning. All the good moorages were taken when we got there. We tied up to a log boom, knowing in a few hours the boats waiting to cross the Sound would be leaving and we could move to the spots they had left. It was still dark when they started their engines, lit their navigation lights, and slid past us with hardly a wake to show they'd passed. I was out on deck watching them go by. There were eight of them: stout, determined boats on their way to somewhere I'd never been. They were the kind of boat I could see Valerie and me fishing from next spring, when, instead of Goletas Channel, we'd be fishing Rivers Inlet.

After moving our boats to moorages the departing gill-netters had left, we slept for a few more hours and then headed back to camp to finally do our canning. Luckily the weather was cool and our fish were still buried in ice by the time we got started. Canning salmon was new to us, and Otto lent us the equipment and pressure cooker we needed for the job. Apparently thinking this gave him licence to supervise, he peppered us with instructions. The cans we were using had to be perfectly clean. The fish had to be cut just right so the lids would fit. The Coleman stove we were using for the canning had to be clear of anything flammable. The pressure cooker was dangerous: if we let the pressure get too high during the cooking process, it could blow up and kill us; if we let it get too low, the fish might be undercooked and develop salmonella and kill us when we tried to eat it later.

When Valerie and I talked it over later, we figured Otto may have come on so strong because Matt had dropped over to watch us. She thought Otto may have taken it as a chance to re-assert himself as our mentor in front of Matt. My taking Matt's advice instead of his on fishing the tides had been a great affront to Otto, she reminded me, and that might have been his try at re-gaining lost ground. Whatever it was, it showed a side of him we'd never seen before. To Valerie, it spoke to Otto's estrangement from his son when his marriage broke up. I just thought it came from getting old and not realizing how he sounded to others. Matt wasn't there to offer an opinion. He'd walked away shaking his head halfway through Otto's lecture.

That day, a Saturday, was the last day Valerie and I spent together in the Duval Point fish camp that season. She had a flight to Vancouver on Sunday and work on Monday. After putting away the fish we'd canned, we kept to ourselves and tried to make the day slow down. We took a load up to the laundry and had a shower. When we got back to the boat, we slid the door of the wheelhouse shut and pulled the trunk cabin curtains closed. We shared some of Matt's wine and got music from the portable radio from a Port Hardy station. Sometime during the afternoon I threw the old wind-up alarm clock on the shelf near our bunk into the fish hold because of its relentless ticking.

That evening we made the rounds as Valerie said her goodbyes to Otto, Matt, and the other gillnetters we had come to know in the camp. Each of them was as tough and independent as any man I'd ever met, but when they heard she was leaving, they couldn't hide their disappointment. Matt had tears in his eyes. What struck me was how quickly the closeness among us had developed. It had been only three weeks since we'd arrived in the camp, and during that time we had been taken in as part of the community. Some of this came from Otto's introductions, although Otto had as many enemies as friends on the docks, and being known as friends of his wasn't always good. It may have had more to do with our willingness to put our inadequate little boat into seas we had no business in. The mix of craziness and ignorance we showed might have been irresistible to some of them— especially the ones who'd started out the way we had. Then again, it may have been simply that Valerie captivated them with her charm, looks, and toughness, all of which she had in spades. Whatever the reason, our new friends were outdoing each other with help and advice. It was as if we had been taken on as a project to make us the best possible gillnetters in the short time we had.

This wasn't at all what we'd been expecting when we headed north. It wasn't hard to see that we were new at fishing and were used to desk jobs. We could handle the physical work, but whether we had the stamina needed to endure four- and five-day openings without any real sleep was the question we had to answer. Why we even wanted to was the bigger question. We already had good jobs. It wasn't lost on us that whatever we caught would be taking away from the catch of someone who didn't have another job to fall back on. It would have been understandable if we'd been ignored or pushed away as interlopers by the real gillnetters, but the exact opposite had happened. It was like we were being welcomed into a big and colourful family.

In the morning, I ran Valerie into Port Hardy to catch her plane. We had a late start, having talked for hours after getting to bed the night before.

The sea in Hardy Bay was flat calm for the trip in. Valerie sat close to me in the wheelhouse. It was her way to not say much when she was thinking about something, and I left her alone.

"I just want you to know I've had a great time up here," she finally said. "The whole camp scene, the people. I'm so glad we went."

"What about next year? You game for crossing the Sound and getting up to Rivers?" I asked.

"Yes, of course. I could see doing this for a while yet." What she meant by that I didn't ask. "But I've had it with that deck pump," she added. "You've really got to get another boat."

8

I fished out of the Duval Point Camp for another three weeks after Valerie left. Each opening I caught slightly fewer fish and saw more boats leaving the camp. My weekends were spent net mending, canning fish, and missing Valerie. Otto and Matt had stayed in the camp as well and we had coffee together every morning we weren't fishing. As usual, they couldn't agree on much, especially about whether we should join the exodus from the camp. Otto was all for it, and talked about his good catches in years past in the Johnstone Strait. Matt said he didn't want to fight the other boats, especially the seine boats out of Port Neville, and would stay in the Duval Point Camp for another few weeks. He said there was usually a late sockeye run in that cycle year and he expected fishing to improve.

After the third week, the Department of Fisheries announced the openings were being reduced from four days a week to three in the Goletas area. That decided it for Otto and me. When I asked Matt if he'd changed his mind as a result of the announcement, he smiled, called the camp his "old man's home," and said he'd be staying.

"No need vorry about Matt," Otto replied when I told him what Matt had said. "I know Matt many, many years. He maybe oldt and lazy, but he alvays know where is fish. He be around to catch last fish in ocean in his net for sure."

That wasn't how Valerie saw it. She'd talked with Matt even more than with Otto. Most of their conversations had been about recipes and cooking tips, but Matt had talked enough about his house and yard in East Vancouver, and how good the first lettuce tasted out of his garden, to give her the impression he was going to retire soon. Matt had been fishing the coast, first on table seiners and then on gillnetters, for over fifty years. There was a sadness that even I detected in his voice about how much the salmon returns had dropped over the years since he'd started fishing. Even when there was a good year or two, the numbers were nothing like the good years he remembered. It was a curse, he told us, to have been doing something for so long that he could see it going bad and know it would never get better. It was the seine boats, he thought, that were killing the salmon fishery, and there was nothing being done by the government to control them.

Although Otto had taught me the most about nets and fishing gear, Matt had taught me the most about gillnetting itself. He was glad to share what he knew and saw the humour in every situation. From what I'd noticed, he was one of the most respected fishermen in the camp. On the day I got back to camp after dropping Valerie off, he was there to help me tie up like he'd done that first time. This time I nudged gently up to the dock and handed him my spring line. He took it with a smile and whipped it into a quick clove hitch.

"So now you handle a boat like a real gillnetter," he said. It was one of the best compliments ever given to me, and one I've never forgotten.

Otto and I left the camp on the Sunday after deciding to part company with Matt. As we passed his boat, there was another whiff of something good cooking, and his arm stuck out his galley window, waving goodbye. The sadness I felt was completely out of proportion for a man I had only known for a month and a half.

We made our first sets off the kelp beds on the west end of Malcolm Island, where Otto said he'd had good luck in years past. We didn't have much luck this time and gave up after three sets, chased out as much by the slamming waves as by the lack of fish.

We finished that week's opening in Johnstone Strait between Growler Cove and Robson Bight. The killer whales seemed to think of the Bight as the place to show their young how to terrorize green gillnetters like myself by heading straight for the net and diving just in time to leave it unscathed. I quickly found out it wasn't worth leaving it set anyway as the sockeye disappeared whenever the killer whales were around, but for a show put on by some of the most impressive animals I'd ever seen, there was nowhere better. Otto got out as soon as the first pod passed and urged me to do the same, saying the orcas would kill and eat me if they had a chance. It was another one of those times I felt badly about disagreeing with him, but something kept me there. I stayed to drift around the Bight, my net safely aboard, for what might have been hours, getting so close to some of the whales I could make out the texture of their wet skin.

Otto had stood by, expecting me to follow him, but when he saw I wasn't coming he'd headed across the Strait to West Cracroft Island and set out among the gillnetters there. I tracked him down later and made a set close by so we could talk if he wanted to. He didn't, so we fished through the night in stubborn silence.

We were saved by our dawn sets. Each of us got a load of fish, and nothing improves moods like picking sockeye out of a gillnet. Our naturally upbeat dispositions returned and we were friends again, but it was plain to see things were never going back to the way they'd been before.

Later that morning, the cash buyers appeared. They were paying two bits a pound more than the companies, and handing out bonuses of forty-ounce bottles of whisky. We delivered our fish and they paid us cash out of battered brief-cases filled with stacks of big bills held together with elastic bands. Otto hesitated about taking his whisky at first, but relented when he read my signal to take it for me. The cash buyers got our fish for the remainder of that opening. Otto gave me his whisky each time, but only after a warning about the dangers of alcohol, re-telling the story of the only time he'd drunk a bottle of beer in some tropical port and been sick as a dog for days afterwards.

We stayed in the area for another week. The fishing became spotty, not helped by an influx of gillnetters from Rivers Inlet and seine boats intent on the Little Adams River run. I could see why Matt wanted to stay in camp and not get mixed up in that sort of fishing. By the end of the week, it had been five weeks since Valerie had left, and Otto was no sub-stitute for her company. He must have felt the same about me compared to the company he'd kept that night in Sointula because he kept suggesting we try the kelp beds off Malcolm Island again. That way we could spend the weekend where there were the showers we both needed and restaurants so we wouldn't have to cook. Otto was such a poor liar I knew exactly what he was really looking to find there. When I jok-ingly asked him her name, he blushed and stammered and finally told me it was Astrid. He asked me never to mention it to Regina or Stephania, as they would both go crazy with jealousy if they found out what he'd been up to. Remembering their send-off party, I could see why he was worried.

Thus reminded of other pleasures in life besides gillnetting, at dawn the next day I wished Otto luck with Astrid and set off for Vancouver.

All went well the first part of the trip. I headed back the same way we had come up and it felt like familiar territory, so I relaxed and enjoyed the scenery. By now there were gillnetters all along the way. Some were anchored in tiny coves off the main channel. A few were travelling, although it looked as if they were frozen in place on the endless waters. Others, farther south where the fishing times were different, were drifting on their sets. Without their splashes of white, the dark green coastline would have seemed more desolate. As I passed their boats, the skippers would wave, and I'd wave back, feeling as though I somehow belonged in this diverse community.

It was new to me, this feeling of belonging to something larger, since most of the things I'd done in my life had been on a solitary basis. I'd grown up more or less as an only child, my sister being my only sibling and eighteen years older than me. As a boy, I had a couple of good friends, but we were more interested in hunting and fishing than running with the other boys in town. Studying architecture, with its long nights of designing buildings and doing presentation drawings, turned out to be as solitary a pursuit as writing. Even when I'd gone abroad, it was to travel alone on my motorcycle, stopping for company only now and then and not for long. It felt good to think of myself as part of the gillnet fleet. What felt better yet was getting closer to Valerie with each passing hour.

In the early afternoon, something in the sound of the engine exhaust changed. I assumed it was my imagination, because stopping to deal with it would have meant abandoning the perfection of the day.

Some people transfer human qualities to inanimate objects like cars or boats, but I'm not one of them. This was why it was so strange that, while ignoring the change in the exhaust sound, payback for my disloyalty to the *T.K.* came into my thoughts. Flashing through my mind were the times I'd seen good-looking gillnetters and wished they were mine. That night standing on the deck of the *T.K.* in God's Pocket watching the gillnetters setting out to cross the Sound was one of those times. Valerie saying we had to get another boat and my agreeing with her and talking about something bigger and newer than the *T.K.* was another. The thought that my boat was getting back at me for my infidelities was laughable, I told myself.

If I'd laughed, it wouldn't have been for long, because in the standing waves where Deer Pass entered Calm Channel, the sound changed again, more ominously this time. Now there was a muted clatter in the exhaust.

Cutting the throttle to half speed, I fought through another half hour of rough water and found a hole at the edge of Calm Channel where I could have a look for the problem. The water pump, my main concern, was still working, but the engine seemed to have more of a vibration than I remembered when I put my hand on it. The temperature gauge had crept up over the past few hours, but I put that down to having the throttle open a little wider as thoughts of Vancouver got into my head. With the engine idling, I noticed it was starting to drop again, but the clatter was still there, coming from deep within the engine block. Then I noticed a different odour in the engine compartment, a burnt smell.

The Gray Marine had been using more oil than usual the past few days. If I hadn't been miles from any settlement, or even if I'd been in a safe anchorage, I might have shut the engine down to check the oil. Instead, I put in a quart and a half while the engine was running, guessing that would be enough to make up what had been used in the day's run.

Back in the wheelhouse, I looked up at the exhaust. It seemed a little whiter than usual, as if there might have been a leak in the main gasket. I still thought there was enough left in the Gray Marine to make it to Vancouver if I took it easy. Setting off again at half speed, the clatter seemed to die away. Little by little, I edged the throttle up to three-quarter cruising speed and held my breath. The temperature gauge crept above normal, but held steady.

Just inside the entrance to Thulin Passage the clatter returned, then changed to a rumble, and the exhaust belched smoke. It sounded like the death rattle of the Gray Marine. I had to get to a dock. Bliss Landing, which I'd just passed, was closest. Lund, up ahead, was farther, but was connected by road to Vancouver. I gambled on Lund. Not daring to raise the throttle above quarter speed, I nursed the *T.K.* along, trailing grey smoke and the stench of burnt oil, and making a racket like an amplified garbage grinder. Finally the Lund dock came into sight. As I drew alongside, the engine gave a shudder that was felt throughout the boat and went silent. After tying up, I pumped the bilge dry, took my pack that I'd made ready the night before, and hurried off to see about a bus to Vancouver.

Following directions at the hotel, I made it, the last person aboard. Seven hours later, I'd had my shower, eaten a meal better than anything I could have found in Sointula, and was drifting off to sleep with Valerie in my arms.

First thing the next morning, I was checking the *Vancouver Sun* for a replacement engine. The plan was to find something as close as possible to the Gray Marine because space in the engine compartment was tight. The time I had to find something was tight too, given the state of the *T.K.*'s garboard seams.

There was nothing in the paper. After a quick breakfast, I was back at the False Creek Fishermen's Terminal. Most of the boats were still up north, but the local regulars were around. The skipper of the *Sloop de Jour* was out having a smoke and poking at the tangled mess of a net on his drum as I walked up. We sort of knew each other, and he was just who I was hoping to see. He wasn't much of a gillnetter, but he was a master scrounger.

Sloop listened to my story of the Gray Marine dying with awe and then pity. A sly look that raised my hopes—and suspicions—crossed his face. He remembered that Wally, a friend of his, was selling a six-cylinder Chevrolet Crusader complete with marine gear for five hundred dollars. It was running fine when he'd taken it out of his boat and put in a new one the previous winter. Sloop knew all this because he'd helped with the work. That was ominous; I'd heard Sloop couldn't even change the spark plugs in his engine. But desperation trumps caution every time. We walked up to the phone together. Wally was home and the engine was still available.

Pretending I didn't know that Sloop would get a cut of the selling price for his trouble, I promised him a case of beer for his trouble.

"I drink high test," he said, referring to Extra Old Stock. "And make it a two-four. That's a hell of an engine you're getting."

I got into Valerie's truck, which I'd brought instead of my car just in case I got lucky, and drove it to Wally's house in Kitsilano. It was a big old place, still clad in Insulbrick. The windows were open and rock music could be heard in the street. Wally might have been deafened by the noise, or more likely negotiating with Sloop about his share of the selling price, because it took him a while to come to the door. He led me out to a garage door in the front of the house and tried six different keys before one opened it. The engine was inside, covered by a canvas tarp. With the cover off, it didn't look that bad. Jumping the starter from a spare battery, Wally had it turning over without any hesitations that might have spelled trouble. It was the moment where you have faith in your luck, or you don't. I did. Having been fool enough to blab out my desperation to Sloop, I knew there was no use trying to negotiate and counted out five hundred dollars.

With the money counted again and in his wallet, Wally raised the engine with a chain lift attached to a house beam and I drove the truck under it. He lowered it onto the same wood blocks it had been sitting on in his basement and I lashed it down, ready for its trip to Lund.

I spent the rest of the day chasing down the tools I thought might be needed for switching the engines. Being new to all this, most of it was decided by guess and instinct. It was an approach that would have appalled my architecture professors, a thought that was satisfying somehow.

As it happened, Valerie's father was in Vancouver. A chartered accountant, he was used to stability in his life. He'd heard about our summer adventures from his daughter. Over dinner, I added the part about the engine dying just as the *T.K.* reached the dock in Lund. He was a Yorkshireman, and tough to read, but I suspect he found what we were telling him hard to believe. To our surprise, he offered to come with us to help change the engine. It may have been just to see what sort of liar his daughter was tangled up with, but I welcomed the help. Valerie was only going to stay long enough to drop off the new engine and have the Gray Marine loaded onto the truck before going back to Vancouver, where she was expected at work. Another set of hands on the winch dropping the new engine into the boat would make the job that much easier. The next morning he crowded into the cab of the truck with us and we headed back to Lund.

Mercifully, the *T.K.* hadn't sunk, but neither would the Gray Marine turn over. A broken crankshaft is what the post-mortem showed, according to the pleasure boater who bought the engine from us later that summer for a hundred dollars less than I paid for the Crusader.

After hand-hauling the *T.K.* to the foot of the winch, we set to work. Detaching the engine from its mounts, shaft coupling, fuel line, and electrical feeds took a couple of hours. Cutting a hole in the wheelhouse roof so it could be winched out took twenty minutes. While I was doing this, Valerie and her father unloaded the Crusader and set it down on blocks on the pier. This allowed the Gray Marine to be dropped into the truck directly after being lifted out of the boat. We snugged it down with the same lines used on the Crusader and Valerie was on her way.

Working out how to shoehorn in the new engine took longer—far longer. Luckily there was a machine shop close by where a bearded old Swede and his bearded young son adapted the old motor mounts for the new engine while I waited. With the mounts loose on the engine bed, I had Valerie's father lower the Crusader down through the hole I'd cut in the wheelhouse roof. Because it was longer than the old engine, I had to tilt the Crusader to squeeze it through while holding the boat steady—a tricky job with the *T.K.* more buoyant than normal without the weight of the engine.

We stopped the Crusader in its descent within a half inch of the mounts. The engine hung there on the thrumming cable while I slid around in the bilge, checking clearances and connections to the shaft coupling and the fuel and electrical systems. Dropping it the final half inch took another two hours while I made sure everything fit. Shimming up the engine for a perfect matchup to the shaft coupling and bolting it down to its mounts took another couple of hours. After that, all that was left to do before starting the new engine was connecting the fuel line and starter wiring. That was going to have to wait because it was now late in the day and we were tired and hungry.

We had supper in the dining room of the Lund Hotel and took our time walking back to the boat. Once aboard, I pulled out one of the bonus whisky bottles and poured us each a shot as a nightcap. We drank to a successful start in the morning and sat on the hatch cover in the warm evening, not talking much and mostly just letting ourselves get sleepy. It was a good feeling. A large measure of it came from how fast things had changed from the moment the Gray Marine had died. It was mostly luck, of course, but there had been a measure of nerve and skill involved. I never would have imagined, let alone tried, an engine changeover like the one I had just done in my previous life. I had to admit it went better than I expected, especially given the crankiness of the *T.K.* Now that I'd been through it, I found I'd enjoyed the work so much I could see myself doing more of that sort of thing, maybe even to the extent of building my own boat one day.

Nearly asleep, I looked the *T.K.* over with a new affection and silently thanked it for its cooperation. Imagining that the death of the Gray Marine was some sort of payback for my disloyalty was laughable in that warm evening air that smelled of the sea. Nothing was going to spoil the Crusader's start-up the next morning.

9

||| UNLUCKY TO THE END |||

For all my confidence in the job I'd done installing the
new engine, I was awakened by second thoughts well before
dawn. Lying in the dark, I went over every step in the instal-
lation process and couldn't think of anything I'd overlooked.
All there was left to do was connect the fuel line, prime the
carburetor, and hook up the starter wiring and instrument
panel. If there was going to be a problem with the start-up,
it would have to be something in the engine itself—and the
involvement of Wally and Sloop meant anything was possible. If worst came to worst and I couldn't solve a problem
myself, the bearded Swedes had a mechanic in their shop
I could call in. I wasn't about to waste time deciding. There
was an opening just announced in the Strait of Georgia that I
was going to make no matter what.

Not wanting to disturb Valerie's father at too early an
hour, I stayed in the bunk until daylight. While coffee was

125

perking on the Coleman stove, I went down into the engine compartment for one last look before making the final connections. Finding everything in order, I laid out the tools I needed and climbed back to the wheelhouse. The coffee was ready and Valerie's father was showing signs of waking. I poured us each a cup and we sat on the hatch cover again. He wasn't a talkative morning person, which suited me because I wasn't talkative at the best of times, especially with my second thoughts about where the engine had come from.

A half hour after we'd finished our coffee, my finger was poised over the starter switch for the new engine. Trying short bursts, I was on the sixth when the engine suddenly caught and purred sweetly. When it had run for ten minutes, I revved it slightly and felt the low rumble of its power. My doubts about the engine vanished and I bid good riddance to the Gray Marine. The thought of fishing the remainder of the season free of all the worries and problems associated with it had me as close to giddy as I'd ever been.

To check out the clutch and transmission, I left the *T.K.* tied up at the dock and shifted into forward gear. The clutch and transmission worked and sounded fine, but the boat went into reverse. When I shifted into reverse, the boat went forward. It was as if the *T.K.* was laughing in my face.

There's no telling what I would have done if Valerie's father hadn't been there. My first thought was a firebombing and the second was a scuttling. All that held me back was not wanting him to think his daughter had taken up with a maniac.

There was no choice but to make the run into Vancouver in reverse. It was a long, tiresome run and I was glad to see Valerie waiting for us when we arrived. While she went to spend some time with her father before seeing him off, I went looking for Harold Clay. I had figured out how to fix my problem and he was just the man to help.

Harold ran Clay's Wharf, home to a collection of raffish live-aboard vessels along the causeway to Granville Island. He made his rounds followed by a trail of pups he called "cockapoos," and was known for his soft heart in hard-luck stories. Mine must have qualified, because he offered to exchange my propeller for one with the opposite pitch, which he was sure he had in his collection. Luckily his ways weren't in use. We guided the *T.K.* into the cradle and he winched it up onto the dry. Using his wheel puller, I had the old propeller off and the replacement he'd found on in an hour. I was beginning to hope that what had started as a catastrophe would end well after all.

Harold had been watching me from the window of his office. When he saw I was done, he came down with his dogs to start the winch to let me back down the ways.

"Your clutch plates are still okay though, eh?" he asked as I petted his dogs.

"Huh? What do you mean?"

"Well, an' I only hearda this once or twice in my life, but when a boat's been run in reverse for too long, the clutch plates can warp."

"I don't know what you're talking about."

"Didn't think you did," he said. "That's why I asked. What I heard is that running a gear revved up in reverse for too long can build up heat and warp the clutch plates. That's because reverse is geared lower than forward. If plates warp, you get creep, meanin the wheel keeps turnin when the boat's in neutral."

"Come on, Harold," I interrupted. "If that's true the net could be sucked into the wheel every time I pick up."

"That's my point," he said in his mild way. "Have you noticed anything? You might tell that the wheel's still pullin when you throw it into neutral. Maybe when you're tyin up," he said.

In fact, I had noticed something of the sort, but hadn't made anything of it at the time.

"So how do you fix it if you have it?" I asked.

"Well, you gotta rebuild the clutch, maybe the gear, I believe. Boat like yours, you'd need to lift the engine out. Why, have you noticed it creeping?"

"Lift the engine out again? No way! I just dropped it in!" I said in disbelief. "Besides, I've got an opening in the morning."

"Hey! Don't get mad at me. I'm just trying to save you a lot more grief if you go fishing like that. You should check it out," he said reasonably.

"Sorry. Okay, maybe I'm wrong. Maybe I'd better check it out again." I had a sinking feeling.

"Okay, get aboard and I'll let you down," Harold said. "You can check when you tie up to the float at the bottom of the ways."

I did, and my worst fear was confirmed. I could see the propeller turning while the boat was in neutral. That meant it would be turning when I brought the net in from a set. Although there was a net-guard under the boat, sections of web could easily be sucked through it into the propeller, seizing it up and rendering the boat helpless. Even if I hadn't heard Otto's stories about skippers getting their net in the wheel and having their boats swept onto rocky shorelines and pounded to bits, I would have realized the danger of fishing with a boat in that condition.

It was a short run back to the False Creek Fishermen's Terminal. Tying up in my berth for the first time in a month and a half brought me back to reality, and the answer came for what to do about the creeping clutch. It was nothing. That damned boat had taken so much of me that I'd reached my limit. I'd keep fishing with it the way it was. When Valerie got back from seeing her father off, we talked it over. She took some convincing, but saw my point. What swung her were the precautions we'd take. First, I'd wire a kill switch into the cockpit. That way I could shut the engine down as soon as the net got too close to the propeller. Even if some of it got caught, I could stop it before too much damage was done. Second, I'd attach a sharp knife to a specially bent shaft to reach under the hull to cut out any web that had been caught in the propeller. Third, I would arrange a tow to safety with Otto or Pete in case I couldn't cut the propeller free. One other thing: there would be a "for sale" sign on the *T.K.* when fishing started in the morning, and my full attention would be on finding its replacement.

We fished the rest of the season, treating the *T.K.* like a ticking time bomb. There had always been a large element of risk associated with that boat and the change in how we treated it now was only incremental. As we got used to the extra precautions, it became a point of pride to have survived each opening. Although there were a couple of times I had to cut out some web caught in the propeller, I didn't have to call for a tow and we didn't lose any fishing time. Not wanting to risk drifting into other boats in case of trouble, we always made our sets a little ways off the main body of gillnetters. The tides often took us even farther, and we'd pick our dawn sets off places like Cape Roger Curtis or the entrance to Porlier Pass. We had some good catches and ran back to the Campbell Avenue fish buyers with the boat heavy with sockeye and, later in the season, chum salmon. Our fishing income that season, without even reaching Rivers Inlet, was more than I earned in an entire year at my day job.

With the season ending, I put ads to sell the *T.K.* into the *Vancouver Sun* and *Province*. By November I had sold the salmon licence separately to someone building a new boat. It took a little longer to sell the *T.K.* itself, but it finally went to a hippie who wanted it for a live-aboard. Despite my warnings about the garboard seams, he spent his time stripping the white paint off the trim and replacing it with oil for a rustic look instead. Within weeks it had sunk in its moorings. It then got pumped out and towed to the seawall near A Float where it sank again. There it lay for months, on its side in the mud in the low tides, and awash to the wheelhouse windows in the high tides until it was nothing but a hulk. One spring morning it wasn't there anymore.

Weeks before I managed to sell the *T.K.*, I had bought our next boat, a newer thirty-four-foot double-ender built by Yamanaka Boat Works in Steveston. The owner had brought it down from Campbell River, and I had taken Valerie to look at it before agreeing to the deal. She was sold on first look, as was I, by its size, beam, and the solid way it sat in the water. The asking price was higher than we wanted to go, mainly because we hadn't realized how much boat prices had risen since I'd bought the *T.K.* But with the seller dropping his price a bit, the proceeds from the sale of the salmon licence, and the remainder from our fishing earnings, we covered it without a bank loan.

One of the first things I liked about this new boat was that the garboard seams weren't an issue; in fact, its bilge was dry. The second was its name, *Ruby Dawn*—far more suitable for a fishboat than *T.K.* The third was its wheelhouse and cabin. Both were much larger than what we'd been used to, and had good headroom. The wheelhouse had a VHF radio and a proper compass and depth sounder. The cabin had a good oil stove and a larger galley with plenty of locker space, but still no head. Even though it was a bit run down and needed a little fibreglass work to fix some deck leaks, I soon had it turned into a real eye-pleaser.

As for a head, I promised Valerie that our next boat would have a proper one, as well as hot and cold running water, and a shower. I wasn't kidding.

10

||| ACROSS THE SOUND |||

"Now ve crossem dat Charlotte Soundt and fishem Riverse Inlet," were Otto's first words when he saw the new boat.

Eight months later, Otto, Pete, Valerie, and I were back in God's Pocket, ready to start the crossing just like Otto had predicted. This time there were eight or nine other boats besides us in the tiny cove. They all reminded me of the ones I'd seen leave that first morning we'd tied up there. The *Ruby Dawn* couldn't match their size or seaworthiness, but was it close, which was more than I ever could have said about the *T.K.*

As Valerie and I settled into our bunk with the alarm set for 3:30 a.m., both of us were too excited to sleep. We talked instead, much like we had the night before Valerie left for Vancouver from Duval Point. There wasn't much to talk about from our trip up this time. Compared to the last year, it was almost boring, but it was just what we needed to understand how long runs on a good boat should go. Along the way we had spelled each other off at the wheel, read, watched the scenery flow by, chatted with Otto on the VHF radio, and even had the luxury of cold watermelon from the two-way refrigerator.

We had been schooled so well by the *T.K.* that we'd started out keeping a suspicious eye on the temperature and other gauges, but seeing them steady hour after hour, we only gave them cursory glances afterwards. The engine, a Chrysler Crown, ran quietly in a well-insulated engine compartment, and we discovered that one of the best ways to make time speed up on a long trip was being able to talk to one another in normal voices. The closest we came to excitement was meeting the flying dog.

It happened in Port Neville. We had stopped there to top up our fuel because the prices were supposed to be the cheapest on the Johnstone Strait. After Otto's shenanigans in Sointula, I half-suspected it was a ploy to meet someone else out of his past. When a woman in a green-checkered flannel shirt came down to the fuel dock from a comfortable-looking house set back among what looked like fruit trees, I was sure of it. It turned out she had a story to tell—one that didn't involve my friend.

A black-and-white dog, a border collie cross of some kind, had followed her down to the dock. The woman started and carried the conversation, as people living in remote places often do with visitors. The dog lay down on the timber deck, never taking his eyes off the woman. As we stood talking, I heard the sound of an airplane approaching in the distance, and the dog began to twitch and whine.

"What's up with your dog?" I asked. "Is it that plane?"

"Is it that plane? Yeah, you might say that." She laughed, as if it were an inside joke. I hate inside jokes, and it may have shown on my face. "Oh, you mean you haven't heard about my dog? This is the famous flying dog of Port

Neville," she said with disarming pride as the dog tried to wrap himself around her legs. "The papers even had a story on him, you know."

Valerie, Pete, Otto, and I looked at each other blankly. "Nope, sorry, we haven't," I said.

"Well!" she began as if this wasn't the first time telling the story.

The previous year, her husband had business in Port Hardy and called in a float plane to take him there. The plane arrived at the same fuel dock where we were standing. The husband said his goodbyes and climbed aboard. His wife noticed that the dog wasn't there when she got back to the house but thought nothing of it. The dog was always tearing off after rabbits and squirrels.

When he landed in Port Hardy, her husband stepped off the plane and saw a dog that looked like the twin to his. This dog looked addled. He was soaked, shivering, whimpering, and barely able to stand. The husband walked past him, but something made him go into the airline office and call his wife. When she told him their dog was still missing, he went out and had a second look at the dog he'd just seen. It was his all right; he could tell by the missing dew claw but not much else. He got a blanket from the pilot and wrapped the dog in it and sat with him. Slowly the dog relaxed and fell asleep.

It must have been a sleep filled with nightmares, because the dog kept whimpering and kicking with all four legs. After an hour of this, he woke up and seeing his master, began to lick his hands and face uncontrollably. For the trip back to Port Neville, the man took his dog on a water taxi.

Afterwards, they pieced together what must have happened. They believed the dog jumped into the water after the pilot had untied the plane's pontoons and climbed into the cabin to start the engine. The woman had their two-year-old son with her and he was acting up, wanting to get down and run around the float. With her attention on him, she hadn't noticed the dog, which must have swum to the pontoon where a canoe was held in place in a special frame, and clambered aboard. Somehow he'd wedged himself into the canoe while the airplane was taxiing out for the takeoff run. He'd managed to stay in place while flying and landing, then jumped out as he saw the plane coming in to dock. The attendant waiting to tie up the plane had said he noticed the dog on the float as the plane was drawing up but didn't know where it had come from.

While the woman was telling her story, the noise of the airplane had peaked and faded as it overflew the entrance to Port Neville on its way west. The dog had lain down again at her feet.

When we were underway again, Valerie asked, "Would you like a dog some day? I would. Maybe even one like that."

"What about Fred? He'd never forgive you," I said.

"Oh, I don't know. He forgave me for you, didn't he? Poor Fred, I know he's lonely."

In those days she would put her cat into kennels when we were up north fishing. The boat I was thinking about building would have enough room to take him with us.

"So how do you think tomorrow will go?" she asked. "Do you think those swells will be as big as Otto says they are?"

"Otto's been known to exaggerate, you know that."

It turned out that he hadn't been exaggerating about the swells we'd encounter, or the dolphins. As we rounded Scarlett Point, they came out, half a dozen or more, to leap across our bows in the kind of send-off he had told us about. Watching them in the growing daylight, we were filled with delight, and any misgivings about the crossing disappeared. According to Otto, the old-time gillnetters believed that dolphins brought good luck for the crossing. They were brave men, but they'd turn back rather than try to make it across if the dolphins weren't there, he said; having luck for that crossing was worth that much to them. From the look of our escort, it appeared we'd be sure to have a good crossing, but then the dolphins disappeared.

The swells gradually built as we made for Pine Island, the first marker of the crossing. We were travelling with Otto a half-net's length away on one side of us, and what looked to be a forty-foot combination gillnet troller the same distance away on the other. The trolling poles on the combination boat were likely thirty-five feet long. Riding the swells, we'd first be looking into a wall of green water below the keel of the combination boat, then open sky above the tops of its trolling poles. Each time we crested a swell, we'd be exposed to the wind off the open Pacific that hit us broadside and caused the boat to broach dangerously before slipping down into the trough between the swells. The cycle continued through the day as we made Egg Island, then Table Island, the other markers of the crossing. Valerie's seat for most of the day was the doorstep so she could look out at the horizon as the rise and fall of the swells permitted. Not one to complain, she didn't let the crossing spoil her record. She did eat all of our dry crackers though—her way of fighting seasickness that had turned her face an exquisite shade of green.

Once inside the sheltering mass of Calvert Island, the swells subsided and our run into Darby Channel and Finn Bay felt like a holiday cruise. Finn Bay was our fishing company's camp in Rivers Inlet. It was much larger than the Duval Point Camp with maybe three times the dock space, more racks for net mending, and a much bigger store. Some of the first people we met after tying up were the friends we'd made in Duval Point the previous year. It was like old times, except that Matt wasn't there, making us wonder if this would be the year he retired. Valerie had to be at the Port Hardy airport before the month was out. We thought we'd leave a little early and visit him on the way. It might be the last time we'd see a great artist at work.

There was enough room along one of the docks for Otto, Pete, and me to tie up in a row. Otto and I had tied up with our stern rollers facing each other so we could go back and forth between our boats easily. The first morning after we arrived was sunny, a rarity in those parts. Valerie and I were sitting out on our hatch cover having a second cup of coffee when we heard a muffled whump from the cabin of Otto's boat. A second later he came charging out the door with a burning camp stove in his hands, the flames licking over his face and head. He threw the stove as far as he could into the bay, where it hissed and smoked before sloping out of sight in the clear water. He looked over at us with his eyes showing all their whites and used his strongest expletive: "My gootness! My gootness!"

We rushed over to help, but he assured us he didn't need any. As we stood talking, he took off his hat to inspect the damage caused by the flames. His face below the line his hat made on his forehead showed the most damage. It was a shiny red and his eyebrows were singed off completely. Valerie offered him some sort of cream, which he applied until his face was white, grinning sheepishly and complaining about how they didn't make those stoves the way they used to. It was his newest one, a mere fifteen years old. Luckily he had spares, four at last count, so it wasn't a major disaster, just an inconvenience because he'd have to fix up one of his spares before he could use it.

Otto refused our offer of coffee and lowered himself into his fish hold where he rummaged around for a good half hour before coming up with a replacement stove and a coil of light line attached to a large horseshoe magnet. Going directly to the rail where he'd thrown the stove overboard, he began casting the magnet out to retrieve it. He wanted it back because it was his best stove, and if he left it in the salt water too long, it would corrode beyond repair, he explained to us as he worked the line. In two hours or so he had the stove drying on his hatch cover while he worked on the replacement stove he'd found in his fish hold. It was so typical of Otto that we had to laugh. He saw the humour and laughed with us. It became the defining moment of our arrival in Rivers Inlet.

Not having Matt around to consult on the best gillnet drifts in Rivers Inlet, I asked Otto where he'd be setting when the fishery opened at six o'clock that Sunday evening. Not surprisingly, he said he'd start on the outside, well offshore where there would be fewer boats, and fewer fish it seemed to me

Pete, who was retired on a good pension and didn't need the money, said he'd fish near him. By now Otto had grown used to my independence and didn't object when I said I'd start near Rouse Reef, where I'd heard there was good fishing. Otto agreed, but told me to be careful I didn't drag my net over the reef itself as there was no telling what I'd dredge up.

I should have listened better. The first gift from the sea that our net hauled in was a pair of giant red jellyfishes. Despite us taking the greatest care, traces of their slime dried on our cuff protectors and aprons and found their way into our eyes long after the jellyfishes themselves were washed overboard. The memory of those stings doesn't fade, no matter how long a person might be away from fishing.

Then came the sea urchins. The bottom of the net had dragged over the reef, just as Otto had warned us against. Rubber gloves were no protection from their erect spines tangled in the net, especially when the net was hauling them up by the hundreds. It looked like they had massed on the reef over the winter and it had been our luck to dredge them up with our first set of the fishing season. I managed to tow the net partly off the reef but the damage was done. The only way I could think to get rid of them was by dropping short sections of net onto the cockpit deck, crushing the urchins, and shaking out the remains. Our gumboots were useless for this as the spines easily drove through the soles. Luckily we had a couple of good-sized pieces of thick plywood, which we used as cutting boards when canning salmon. Using them to protect our feet, we stomped around the cockpit deck like demented grape crushers.

The urchin remains left the cockpit, and a wide area of water around the boat, covered in a mustard yellow skim of urchin roe that gave off a strong fishy smell, attracting every seagull in the vicinity. In France, sea urchins were considered a gourmet delicacy. They were served on ice, turned upside down onto their spiny backs. Their bottoms were cracked open in the manner of boiled eggs, and the roe was eaten with small silver spoons. Here they were gourmet delicacies only to the seagulls, many of them swimming after the boat with their white breasts stained yellow from gulping down the floating roe.

Despite the jellyfish and urchins, there were thirty sockeye in our net. In our next sets, farther in from the reef, there were more, and we began to appreciate why Rivers Inlet had such a reputation among gillnetters. Although we were new to the area, we kept finding good drifts. By the time that first week's fishery closed, we had topped our previous best week in Duval Point for sockeye, although there were only a couple of smileys in the lot.

Maybe it was Valerie's new master of anthropology degree, none of which showed in her easy-going manner, but she was even more intrigued by Finn Bay than she was by Duval Point. It was much larger for one thing. It felt more comfortable being there. If nothing else, we were no longer the menaces we were when I couldn't dock the *T.K.* properly, or didn't have the sense to wait out a big storm passing through. We spent a lot of our weekends on the docks meeting new people and just looking around. The docks at this camp were much wider than those at Duval Point, leaving plenty of room for people to pass alongside the net racks set up in the middle. My nets always needed work, leaving me in a good position to talk to other skippers and the passersby. Valerie, with her laundry and shopping trips, and her friendly nature, soon had a circle of friends she could have spent the day chatting with if she'd wanted to.

The camp was really a community that lasted from the first fishery opening in May until the last fishery closure in the fall. It had its solid citizens and its outsiders. I was more interested in the outsiders: the hippie enclave, the old Japanese men on well-kept wooden boats, the Croatians and Italians with awnings up and wine on tables set up on their decks, and the old drunks spending the summer in the camp not so much to fish as to get away from their wives.

Valerie saw it in the larger sense, likening it to a typical small town in those days, except for being afloat. As with any small town, there were the pillars of the community. In Finn Bay they were the skippers, usually with their wives as deckhands, who had fished for the company since the 1950s and even earlier. The skippers tended to their nets, looked after their boats, and drank with their buddies when allowed by their wives. When fishing, the men were in charge, but on the docks, the women were. With their men organized for the day, the women visited back and forth in small groups over tea and coffee, out on their decks or in their cabins depending on the weather. It was with these groups that Valerie often stopped for a chat. They were formidable women, some of whom we'd already met in the Duval Point Camp. Being in fishing, they were familiar with tragedies in their lives. One day Valerie told me about a woman she had heard about in one of these groups who had lost her grandson at sea.

The boy had been with his grandparents on their boat heading for Rivers Inlet a few years back. The grandparents, who had fished all their lives, had been looking after him for the summer and had started taking him fishing with them. He loved it. They kept a close eye on him from the start, but he had turned out to be a sensible boy and they relaxed a bit seeing that.

The year they lost him they had let him sit on deck with his lifejacket on to read comic books in the shelter of the cabin. The grandmother had checked on him from time to time and found all was well. She brought him out a snack and then went back and collected the dishes and leftovers. After washing up and talking with her husband for a while, she went out again and he wasn't there. The lifejacket was lying on the deck where he had been sitting, but he was gone. She screamed to her husband. He immediately doubled back down the straight line of the boat's wake. It was a fast boat and they covered a lot of ground, but they couldn't find him. They radioed for help as soon as it happened, but it was slow arriving. Long before it came, they knew he'd been lost in that cold water. What had likely happened was that he had taken off his lifejacket to have a pee over the side of the boat and had fallen in. He wasn't much of a swimmer, and without the lifejacket, he didn't have a chance of survival.

After the search ended, they went back to Vancouver to break the news to their daughter. They stayed with her and didn't fish that year. The following year they were back in Rivers Inlet.

"You just have to live with it," the woman said. "What else can you do? We can't quit fishing. It's how we live."

Valerie was taken by the calm way in which the woman had spoken about what had happened, and how she could go on talking about other things. From the looks of the women in her group, she could see how they would have helped her deal with the tragedy. That year there were a few young boys running around the docks, which must have made it more difficult for them all.

One of the boys was the grandson of a couple we knew mainly because of my efforts to fish near his grandfather, who was the camp's highliner. I was hoping to learn some of his tricks. He had noticed my efforts and made a game out of escaping and then teasing me about it after. One day he invited me for coffee. I didn't need more of an invitation to ask him about himself. When I tried, I could see where his talent for evading me on the fishing grounds came from. He did mention that in the off-season his job was to station his boat in the middle of the Skookumchuck rapids and wait for the tide change. When he saw it happen with his own eyes, he would radio the tugboat skippers standing by with gravel scows so they'd have the safest chance for getting through the dangerous passage.

I also found out that he started every day in a freshly washed shirt, still warm from the iron. His wife, after whom his boat was named, had been doing this for him since they were married. She did so whether they were tied up in camp with laundry facilities, or out on the fishing grounds where she used a galvanized washtub and an iron heated on the stove. His wife, a Native woman, was even harder to get anything out of than he was, but their grandson made up for the two of them.

He told me he was along to collect beer bottles from the boats tied up in the camp. It was his second year doing this. The first year he had returned a load that had completely filled his grandfather's fish hold. It had made him nearly two hundred dollars. So far this year he was doing even better. It was a hardship to his grandfather because he could only use his side lockers for his catch, meaning he had to call in the collector several times a day. In return, he had to wash the salt spray from the boat whenever they came back in from an opening and get good marks in school. He was living up to the bargain. Unlike the other young boys, he never seemed to be idle and he gave the impression he would go on to do big things with his life.

The fishing was good that summer. Otto and Pete decided to stay on when Valerie and I left for Port Hardy. Our plan was to fish out of Duval Point Camp with Matt for a week before she had to catch her plane. Crossing the Sound was a calmer passage than on the way up, but we did see a gillnet boat that had foundered. We got close enough to see its name, the *Sea Otter*. From the seaweed growing on it, we gathered that it had been there a while.

We got into Duval Point Camp just in time to surprise Matt at his late supper, and were invited aboard joyfully. He drew out a fresh gallon of his homemade wine from under his bunk and poured drinks into tumblers. While we drank, he threw some more salmon steaks onto his still-warm frying pan and soon we were eating together. When we told him what we were planning, he thanked us and told us to keep an eye on him about noon on the last day of the opening. He'd be picking the last set of his life about then and heading home. He was right on schedule, but I almost didn't live to see it.

We stayed up late that night listening to Matt talk about his life and slept in the next day, the start of the next week's fishery. It was a three-day opening, surprisingly short for that time of year according to Matt. There weren't many boats in camp, and we had no trouble finding spots to fish alongside Matt. He didn't use the radios in his boat, so we tied up a scotchman to the end of our net and idled over to his boat so we could talk some more. The good weather we'd had in Rivers Inlet had followed us down to Duval Point and we were in the phony cheerful state that sometimes happens before big changes in life. The nets behaved and it was nearly two hours later that we picked them. We had about sixty sockeye and Matt looked like he had double that.

As usual, we stayed out and fished through the night while Matt went into camp for his rest. The pattern continued until the last day of the opening. Matt had been coming out later and later to make the midday slack tide and we could see that he'd planned his last set for it. That left us the whole morning to fish on our own. We were tired from fishing through the night, but not so bad that I was "thinking like a baby," as the Croatian fishermen called the fatigue that set in during the last days of a long opening. The sea was unusually calm and we were on our own along the south shore of Goletas Channel where we'd had good luck in the past. The net had been down for over an hour when I put on my apron and cuff protectors and went to pick it. After pulling the end of the net close to the boat, I watched myself put the boat in reverse as if in an out-of-body experience and run it up into the net until the propeller stopped turning and the engine stalled. Having avoided something like this on the *T.K.*— that floating accident waiting to happen—I somehow had managed to do it on a boat that was far safer.

If we'd been a little farther off shore, I might have called the fishing company for a tow to somewhere safe where a diver could be brought in to clear up the mess. It would have been the smart thing to do if there had been time. From my read of how quickly the tide was carrying the boat and net toward the beach, though, we were past that chance. The boat was too beamy to reach into the propeller from above with a knife lashed to a pole. My only choice was to dive under and cut out the net by hand. I stripped down to my shorts, spent a few minutes re-sharpening my sharpest knife, clamped it into my teeth like Tarzan, and dove in. My last glimpse of Valerie was her standing at the rail, her mouth open in horror, holding her hands clasped like the heroines in the old movies when a train was advancing on her boyfriend lashed across the tracks.

I had to come up for air three times, but managed to cut the last of the net free just as things were turning black. My back scraping along the hull seemed to wake me up and give me the energy to reach the surface and breathe again. The water, shockingly cold, had stiffened me up so badly that I wouldn't have been able to get back aboard without Valerie. I might not even have tried all that hard if I had been alone. The water was feeling warmer by then, and seemed to be gently inviting me for one last dive into its blue-green depths. It wasn't until I was lying on deck, wrapped in towels and a sleeping bag with Valerie on top adding her warmth, that I came back to myself.

As I lay there, feeling the boat rock gently on the deceptively benign water, I remembered Otto's stories of boats being found adrift with no one aboard. What had sounded so fantastic coming from him at the time now seemed possible—even likely. Death would have come casually if I'd been alone. Another story would have been added to the ones about boats found adrift with their skippers lost. Of all the differences between gillnetting and ordinary life, it was clear to me now that the greatest was the acceptance of death's proximity on the water.

Two cups of coffee spiked with Hudson's Bay rum revived me enough to join Valerie picking the net. By the time we were done, we could hear the gentle lapping of water on the rocks of the shoreline that we likely would have been trying to save the boat from if we'd been a half hour later.

As it turned out, we had a nice load of sockeye aboard, and a net that needed mending but was safe on the drum, and we made it back to see Matt make his last set. We saw his boat slowly come out of the camp entrance and head toward us. Valerie and I were sitting on the hatch cover with fresh coffee after making another set. I had taken advantage of the calm seas to square off the torn section of net that might have got caught in the wheel again. Matt stopped his boat a few feet from ours and came out on deck.

"Would you like a coffee, Matt?" I yelled.

"Thanks, but no!" he shouted back. "I came to cork you! You can't cork me back because this is gonna be my last set!"

Before I could reply, he ducked stiffly into his wheel-house and wheeled off.

"I think he's crying," Valerie said.

A net's length away, Matt began his set. Once it was made, he went into his wheelhouse, even though it was a fine day, and didn't come out again until he was ready to pick his net. We had begun picking ours by then. We finished at about the same time he did. People said Matt would catch the last fish swimming, he was that good of a gillnetter. On that set, his last ever, he might have caught thirty, a fraction of what he was used to. We could see from how low his boat was riding that he'd packed ice and would be taking his last catch home. When the net was in, he pulled his scotchman up over the rollers. Swinging it around and around over his head like a lasso, he then slammed it down onto the deck at his feet.

"That's it! Goodbye forever!" he shouted into the wind.

Valerie was right; he was crying.

Giving us a long wave, he pointed his boat toward Johnstone Strait and Vancouver. It was the most impressive retirement I've ever seen.

We still had fishing to do before heading into Port Hardy and the airport, but we watched his boat get smaller for a long time before starting our next set. Matt used to say that of all the ways to fish for a living on the West Coast, the best one for old men and dreamers was gillnetting. Even in our short time gillnetting, we'd seen days where the water was like glass, our net-corks curving out behind the boat for nearly a quarter of a mile among reflections of cedar-clad mountains and rocky beaches. The only disturbance would come from fish hitting the net, causing the corks to bob and send ripples out into the mirror. Some nights in Rivers Inlet when it was clear, the lights of our mast and net would be lost among thousands of others, and looking into the distance it was hard to tell where the fishing lights ended and the stars began. Matt was crying about the times like these that he would never see again.

With Matt, and especially Valerie, gone, the next few weeks were difficult. The weather turned bad and boats began heading toward Vancouver where there was talk of a big return on the Fraser. Remembering Matt's words about a late sockeye run off Duval Point, I stayed in the camp. Otto and Pete showed up to overnight and then joined the parade south. I stayed on for another week, but there was no sign of the return Matt had talked about. It might have been an old man's myth. I left the camp sad about that, but what I had on the dash soon cheered me up. They were sketches of a new boat that I had drawn in the lonely days just after Matt and Valerie left.

11

||| **THE REAL RHONDA** |||

For the first time in over two months, I slept at home. It was now early September, three years after we'd bought the *Ruby Dawn*, and I was just back after the summer's fishing. My last stop after weeks in Rivers Inlet was Growler Cove in Johnstone Strait, where I'd had a whack at the tail end of the sockeye bound for the Fraser River. I was finally getting the hang of gillnetting and the season was going well. There were still a few openings left around the Fraser River and maybe some fall fishing after that. If my luck held, this was looking like it could end up the best year by far since I'd started fishing five years ago.

The timing couldn't be better. Valerie and I were in the midst of changes in our lives—and those changes cost money. For one thing, we were now married. For another, we'd bought a house, a small one in East Vancouver, and there was a mortgage to pay every month. And yet another, there was a new boat in our future. I was planning to build it myself, which meant I wouldn't be going back to my architectural job until after next year's fishing season. We'd be living on what Valerie made at her job as a social worker, and rent from the tenants in our basement suite.

The new boat was going to be fibreglass with a Detroit Diesel engine, thirty-seven feet long, fast, beamy, and seaworthy enough for offshore fishing. I'd be starting with what was called a "kit," consisting of the hull, cabin, and decks laid up and assembled by a company called Deltaga Boatworks. I would do the rest of the work myself. When finished, it was going to be a combination boat equipped with a gillnet drum and stern rollers, and trolling gear—four spool gurdies, thirty-two-foot poles, and rigging.

Most of the new boats were going this route because the Fisheries Department had started cutting down gillnet openings and breaking up the coast into smaller areas where the openings were at different times. Faster boats had an advantage when travelling between the different areas with their different opening times. Combination boats allowed the skippers to switch to trolling when gillnetting was closed in those areas. Our new boat, with its speed and trolling gear, would let us do either. What's more, the comforts I was building in, like a full galley, oversized bunk, and separate head with sink, shower, and a hot-water system would make the long hours and hard work more bearable.

The deposit on the kit had been paid, a place where I'd do the rest of the work in the Deltaga yard had been reserved, and a delivery date had been set. We had money put aside for the final payment on the kit, and what I estimated it would cost to finish the boat would come from selling the Ruby Dawn. I had a construction schedule drafted that said if I worked fourteen hours a day six days a week for eight months, the boat should be ready for sea trials in late May.

Never having attempted anything even close to this in the past, it was based on pure speculation and, of course, luck.

In order to give the proposed schedule any kind of a chance, I gave myself two weeks to find a salmon licence big enough for the new boat. If I couldn't find one by then, I'd have to take up time meant for building it. Licences were getting to be in short supply because of all the new boats being built. It meant weeks could be lost off the construction time, putting next year's fishing with the new boat in jeopardy. I wasn't a worrier by nature, but it was seldom far from my thoughts that finding a licence in time was an even weaker part of the overall plan than my stab at the construction schedule.

Pete and Otto were waiting for me in front of the *Ruby Dawn* when I got there about mid-morning the day after I came home. They had phoned the house and Valerie had told them when to expect me. I had last fished with them in Rivers Inlet, but they had left early and had been tied up in their berths on A Float for a couple of weeks. They'd just heard some tragic news, which made them think of me, or that was how they began what they wanted to tell me.

Lou, one of the gillnetters who'd tied up at the end of our float, was in hospital dying of cancer. The tragedy was that he had no family or friends and he was dying alone. There was the matter of his boat, which was why they thought of me. Otto and Pete heard that an ex-wife or girlfriend had his power of attorney and she was trying to sell the boat cheap and fast. By pacing it off, they'd figured the licence on that boat could be stretched out to fit the boat I was building. They didn't have to say anymore. I thanked them, and started for the wharfinger's office to see if I could find out where this ex-wife or girlfriend lived so we could talk business.

I remembered Lou from the first year I tied up at the False Creek Fishermen's Terminal, mainly because he didn't look like a gillnetter. He was small and slight with the pallor of a convict. His clothes were straight from Army & Navy: black nylon jacket zippered to the throat, black pants, slippery-looking black loafers, and a narrow-brimmed grey fedora that might have looked jaunty on someone else. I'd see him hurrying back and forth on the float several times a day. Sometimes he carried a shopping bag from Safeway. He wouldn't look you in the eye when he passed, and answered with a quick nod when you said hello. His manner reminded me of a couple of pool sharks I knew, small-time hustlers in the pool halls on East Hastings Street. Like them, he was never without a cigarette in his mouth.

None of my friends on the float knew much about him. They knew he was called Lou, and his boat was named the *Rhonda*. He did his fishing around Labouchere Passage, which they called "Labasher." His nickname was "lost cause Lou," and it had something to do with a woman, but that was about all they knew, and seemed interested in knowing. One morning I gave in to my curiosity when I saw him rushing by and went to look at his boat. You could learn a lot about a man by looking at his boat. I found it among the workboats, small tugs, and hippie boats tied up close together in a sort of floating slum.

The *Rhonda* was as odd a boat as its owner was a man. About thirty-five feet long and carvel planked, the hull had an odd roundness that likely meant crankiness in any kind of a cross-sea. Despite that, there were no stabilizers. The low main cabin sat directly on the deck amidships with no trunk cabin or wheelhouse. The cabin top was rounded like a gypsy wagon and the windows, three across the front and one at each end of the sidewalls, were curiously arched. A canvas-covered hatch cover took up most of the short rear deck. The drum was wooden and had a net on it that looked bleached by the sun. The checkers on either side of the drum were small and the control station was ancient. Wooden stern rollers that were showing their age sat on a square stern that closed in a short cockpit. The work light was nothing more than a bare bulb in a black rubber socket dangling from a bent aluminum pipe attached to the stern rollers. Fish scales and grime were caught in all the corners that were harder to reach, and a faint smell of something rotten came up from that end of the boat.

It looked as though the hull had once been painted white, the decks and cabin roof grey, and the trim dark green, but the lack of maintenance had made it hard to tell. A short stovepipe with a rain cap stood on the starboard side of the cabin roof near the door. A layer of soot spread outward from the stovepipe, covering every surface with a thickness in proportion to its distance from the source. The only disturbance to this pattern was a trail of footprints leading from the sisal mat outside the door around the hatch cover and over to the rail where Lou obviously came and went. Black streaks ran down the hull from the deck scuppers to the waterline. Thick brown curtains, pulled completely closed, covered each window. At night, when the owner was inside with a light on, a dull brownish glow might have been all that showed through the windows.

Neglected old wooden fishboats reek of stove oil, bearing grease, bilge slime, and wood rot. The smell engulfs bedding, cushions, clothing, and the person living aboard. The Rhonda smelled like that, intensely, with overtones of raw gasoline and stale cigarette smoke. It was a sad, hopeless smell that I'd noticed trailing off the little man when I passed him on the float. Rundown fishboats were usually the victims of benign neglect, often by owners who couldn't do the work needed anymore. With the Rhonda it seemed more than that. It was almost as if the neglect was somehow malicious. It was hard to imagine what sort of person would do that to his boat. The thought of buying a boat like that turned my stomach, but it sounded like a chance to solve my licensing problem.

The wharfinger had the ex-wife's address as the person to notify in case of emergency. It turned out that the boat was named after her, of all things. Before heading out to find her, I went down to see if anything about the *Rhonda* had changed. If it had, it was for the worse. It was lying deeper in the water, sootier than ever, the brown curtains still drawn over every window. I'd taken a tape measure from the *Ruby Dawn* and found the length to be thirty-five feet, eight inches.

My new boat was going to be thirty-seven feet long. According to the rules, a licence from a retired boat could be applied to a new boat of the same length. Measurements in those days were done with hand-held tape measures with a fisheries officer holding one end of the tape, and the boat owner the other. It was understood that the fisheries officers allowed some leeway when measuring. With luck, the licence from the *Rhonda* could be stretched just enough to match my new boat. That was good enough for me. I headed off to meet the real Rhonda, stopping at the bank on the way.

The bank opened at ten in the morning and I was the first one in. My request to withdraw twelve thousand dollars in large bills caused the teller to call the manager. He strongly suggested a certified cheque, but something told me Rhonda was a cash-up-front sort of person. I left with a wad of bills as thick as a good steak. Not knowing how much she would be asking, I had to be ready for anything. Twelve thousand dollars was a few thousand less than the going rate for the size of licence she was selling. I thought it would be a fair opening offer because the boat itself was worthless, a liability if anything. If it came down to it, I was prepared to go a bit higher, to avoid haggling with a soon-to-be-grieving widow.

Rhonda's address was in East Vancouver on Fourteenth Avenue near Trout Lake park. It turned out to be a small stucco bungalow with a picture window, hip roof, and a raised basement like hundreds of houses built in the early '50s. This one had been let go. The glass fragments in the stucco didn't glitter in the morning sun as they would have if the walls had been even halfway clean. The most recent paint job, pea green, was flaking off the eaves and window trim, showing the original ivory colour underneath. A sixty-foot balsam fir in the front yard threw enough shade that moss had defeated grass years ago in the battle for the front lawn. The front walk led up to concrete steps flanked by hydrangea bushes with a few bluish flowers on them. Yellowing flyers sheltered under them like chicks under a mother hen. The front door had an aluminum storm door with a torn screen and the outline of a flying mallard on the bottom panel. Two aluminum mail-boxes with nothing in them were attached to the stucco wall beside the door. Doorbell buttons were mounted beside them. A faded, hand-printed sign under one of the buttons said "Rhonda—rear." I pressed it several times, suspecting it didn't work, then headed around to the back of the house.

A narrow concrete sidewalk, nearly crowded out by one of the hydrangeas, angled through a wooden archway with a missing gate, and ran along the side of the house to the back-yard. The sidewalk was algae-covered and slippery, and the air reeked of tomcat spray. At the back of the house there were two sets of stairs: one up to a small porch and one down to the basement level. The stairs down to the basement had a small gabled roof over them and a bare light bulb still burn-ing. I went down and knocked on the door. After my fourth knock, a sleepy-sounding woman somewhere in the depths of the house said, "It's open." In two words, her voice gave away a close familiarity with smoky bars and cheap whisky, but I was still surprised by what I found inside.

The door opened into a passageway with cases of empty beer bottles stacked four high along one side. It was dim and the place smelled of stale beer and cigarette smoke, like the beverage rooms on Cordova Street. I passed a closed door, then made out a sitting room on the left and a kitchen on the right. Beer bottles, a few whisky and wine bottles, glasses, potato chip bags, pizza boxes, and loaded ashtrays filled the kitchen table and countertops. A table lamp burning in the far corner of the sitting room showed more of the same on the coffee and end tables. The windows in the suite were small, set high in the walls, and closed off by venetian blinds. Enough light came through to outline more bottles standing on the sills. I was standing in either the remains of a monstrous house party, or poor housekeeping of catastrophic proportions, or both.

As I stood there, peering around in amazement, a light went on behind a half-closed door to the right of where I was standing. Bedsprings creaked, there was some rustling, a lighter clicked open and closed, and someone took a rasping drag on a cigarette. Country music came on. The light spilling out was pink.

"So, you comin in or what?" she said.

I pushed the door open and stepped into the pink glow. A queen-size bed took up most of the room. A red satin cover was pushed to one side, exposing pink shiny-looking sheets. The bed had an arched headboard upholstered in tufted pink satin with round, white studs around the edges and small heart-shaped mirrors in the upper corners and top of the arch. On the sheets, a blond woman in a sheer black negligee reclined in the classic pose of nudes painted by the Renaissance masters. The pose was the only thing classical about her; everything else matched the headboard. Her mouth dropped open in surprise when I walked in, but it didn't take her long to recover. She had already shifted her position to show more cleavage and less stomach, sizing me up all the while.

"Well, hello," she rasped. "What's your name?" She emphasized the "your" like vamps used to do in old black-and-white B movies.

"John Smith," I shrugged. "What else?"

She laughed at that. Thirty years ago it would have tinkled; now it sounded like gravel sliding down a steel chute.

"A wise guy—I like you already. Come and sit down beside me." She patted a spot on the bed beside her.

She took another drag on the cigarette and blew the smoke at me playfully. There was still liquor on her breath, and a coarse smell of perfume and body odour rose from her bed. Here she was, haggard after what must have been a hard night, pushing sixty from the look of her—even in that flattering pink light, awakened by a stranger in her house, and she was ready to party. If nothing else, she had stamina.

"How about a beer?" She reached down into an open case in front of her imitation French-provincial night table. "I'm gonna have one."

She brought two bottles out. They clinked against each other merrily over the sound of the music. There was an opener on the night table that she used with a practised hand. She held the bottle out to me with a little foam running down the neck. It seemed like the most natural thing to do in that situation at eleven o'clock in the morning, so I took it.

"You must be Rhonda. Here's to you," I said, saluting her with the bottle.

"Why thank you." She gave me a smile she must have learned watching the vamps in those old movies. "Come and sit down, shy boy." She patted the spot beside her again.

There was nowhere else to sit in that room, and I did feel a little awkward standing there with my bottle of beer, but sitting down beside her on that bed was out of the question.

"I'm a prude," I told her and kept standing.

"Hah! I bet!" she said. "You know, hon, all my visitors come into my bed. They never regret it, but I guess you're here for something else." Her face suddenly changed and she looked at least eighty. I thought she might cry.

For the first time she looked away from me and gazed vacantly around the room as if she was a stranger there herself. Her eyes stopped at a Mexican sombrero that was hanging incongruously on the wall. She studied it for a moment then gave her head a little toss, as if dismissing what had come into her mind, and turned back toward me.

"I guess you've come about the boat."

She put her cigarette down into the butts filling the ashtray on her bedside table and put her beer down beside it. She swung her feet off the bed, showing all of her still-not-bad legs, and got into a pink chenille housecoat that had been thrown over a pile of clothes on a chair next to the bedside table. She lit another cigarette and squirmed up to sit against the headboard. It looked like she was ready to talk business.

"Poor Louis," she said, shaking her head. "He's not too good. I was up to see him the other day but he didn't want me around. Doesn't want anybody around, not that anybody would want to see him. He's too weak to get out of bed by himself. You know, they got him in this room with three other guys all dyin of the cancer." She looked at the cigarette in her hand and crushed it into the ashtray. It continued to smoke away but she didn't notice.

"We only made it up to Hardy this year. Never did much fishin. He wasn't up to it, and I don't handle the net. Came back down in July and he went to the doc. I can't ever remember him doing that before. They put him inta St. Paul's right away. Then they said there was nothin they could do for him and were going to send him home with some painkillers. When they found out he only had the boat to live on, and I sure as hell didn't want him here, they kept him there. He's been there ever since. He don't want no visitors. Don't want anybody to see him the way he is.

"You might not believe it lookin at me, but I used to go up with him every year. I'd cook, clean up a bit, polish the stove, just keep him company. You should see the stove—it is some shiny. An' I got friends up and down the coast that I visit. Louis drops me off and picks me up. I like to party. He doesn't—he hates it. He hardly drinks. I do. He smokes, though. God, does he ever, or used to anyway. I used to roll 'em for him on his little machine. I'd make up a couple a hundred at a time; might last him a day or two.

"He wouldn't live here; too many parties. An' like I told you, any man comes through that door comes into this bed. You're about the first one that didn't. I'm a rounder, that's what I am. Used to be at the Sunrise Hotel, you know the Sunrise on Hastings Street? That's where I used to be. I had me a front room lookin out over Hastings. I don't know why I'm blabbin like this; it ain't your kind face, that's for sure. That was a joke, hon. Oh, yeah, siddown on that chair, just throw that stuff on the floor. Anyhow, there was me an' a coupla other girls; rounders, that's what we were. Loved the parties, we did. We'd go anywhere. I ended up in a loggin camp one time. Even the cops liked us, but we put out for them too. Sure we did. They used to tell us about their mean wives, real bitches. Things were different then. Everybody knew everybody, knew what they was about and left them alone. Ain't like that now though; it's all goin to hell, really. I'm the only one I know that don't lock the door.

"Ahh, I'm gonna miss Louis. Don' know what I'm gonna do in the summer. How much did you say that boat was worth?"

I hadn't said, but this time I told her. She lit another cigarette and thought it over.

"You know, I don't recall seeing you up in the camps. You, I woulda remembered. You only go up to Rivers? Oh, we used to go there, up to Bella Bella, Labouchere, Milbanke, all them places. Less boats, easier fishin. Louis knew them places like the back'a his hand. Never used a compass or them maps, just knew where he was goin. He made a lot of money with that little boat, hard to believe but true. Named her after me, eh. Some guy around Nanoose Bay built 'er. Didja see them fancy windows? Louis wanted them like that; said they reminded him of a church in the town he came from. Actually he's from the prairies, a farm there somewhere. He used to go into that town for some fun, an' to get away from his old man.

"He was a mean old bugger, the old man, used to beat him up, him an' his mother. The war came an' he went into the army. Never talked about it, but some guys I ran into one time knew about him an' said he did good. Even got some kinda medals; I never seen them though. Anyway, the war ended an' he wasn't going back to no farm. He came out to the coast. Went deckhandin for a while on one a them old table seiners. Hard work. Skipper reminded him of his father, so he quit. He rented a boat and went gillnettin after that. Liked it an' stayed with it. Twelve thousand you figure, eh? Got it with you? Let's see it."

I reached over and put the money on the bed and she riffled through it thoughtfully. Our beers were finished by now. She opened two more and lit another cigarette.

"Ya know, it's been thirty years since Louis an' me been together. Not that we were all that together. Not married or anythin like that, but he's been kinda lookin after me. God knows I need it. It was in Nanaimo him an' me met, in a bar, where else, eh? He was headin up north for the season in that old double-ender he rented, an' I was over visitin my girlfriend. We ended up in the Legion, Louis an' me. He was good-lookin then, and drank a bit. I woke up on his boat. Don't remember gettin there, but I couldn't get off; he was already on his way up north. So what the hell, I stayed with him that whole summer. Ended up I didn't mind it at all. Made some money. Had some laughs. Went back to Vancouver that fall an' moved in together. It lasted for a while but then we got to fightin pretty regular. He got that boat around then an' called her the Rhonda, after me, eh.

"Oh, it was the damndest thing, we could live together pretty good out fishin but get back to town an' it was fight, fight, fight. He never liked me havin all' a them friends, ya know? But he knew what I was like, an' I never tol' him I was gonna change. He knew what he was gettin. Yeah, I like to party all right. Been doin some'a that here the last few nights. Some'a the guys that knew Louis were even here, but it ain't the same now he's so sick. Our hearts ain't in it. Mine ain't anyhow. Don't know what I'm gonna do when he's gone. He's always looked after me, like I just said. See this place, he pays the rent. I been thinking about movin downtown again, but everybody I used to know down there is gone. Moved away, or more likely died, I guess."

She looked around as if sizing up the job of moving all her stuff, and ended up looking at the sombrero again.

"I dunno why I'm sitting here blabbin like this. It ain't really like me, but you see that Mexican stetson there, I got it in Mexico. Louis took me there one winter. He came down with the runs pretty bad, but me, I had a hell of a good time. Met some friends of John Wayne's even. They was down fishin for marlin or somethin. Took me out on their boat, an' it was nothin like the Rhonda, I can tell ya. Treated me like a movie star. There was a couple of other girls aboard that thought they was movie stars by the way they acted, but I was better lookin than any of 'em. You shoulda seen me thirty years ago, you woulda been only too happy to sit down on my bed. I was a looker, a real looker; they said I looked like Betty

Grable. Louis sure was mad when I got back, but he was so sick he couldn't do anything about it, poor bugger. That's one of the times he took off on me when we got back to town here.

"Hell, I didn' care at the time. I had some'a them fancy uptown guys, stockbrokers or somethin, lookin me up. Don't kid yourself, I've ridden in Cadillacs. I even rode in a Mercedes-Benz once, but Caddies are my favourite though. Did you know Hank Williams died in the back of one? You did? Hah, a lotta people don't know that, but that would be a way to go, wouldn't it? One guy even had a pink one, my favourite colour. He woulda let me drive it too, but I couldn't drive. Never got a licence. I'm sorry about that now, but back then I used to get rides everywhere. Now I gotta take a bus. Taxis got too dear, eh.

"So what papers do I gotta sign? We gotta go to a lawyer's? I hate them bastards. Never helped me any, an' I've seen a few of 'em, I can tell ya. Hated 'em all. Guess I better get dressed then. Where ya goin? You can stay and watch if you like, I don't mind."

Waiting for her in the kitchen, I found a telephone among the party leftovers and called my lawyer so he would be ready for us. He was a friend of mine who had skippered a collector boat for one of the fishing companies to put himself through school. Before starting to get dressed, Rhonda dug around in her purse and handed me an envelope of boat documents. It contained a power of attorney in her name with a signature by Lou that was nothing but a shaky scribble. That and the other papers in the envelope looked like all we'd need to make the sale official. A few minutes later, Rhonda made her entrance in red heels and a short red dress with a plunging neckline.

"You like?" she said, giving her hips a shimmy.

"Very nice," I said, imagining the effect she'd have in my friend's law office.

She went into the bathroom to put on her face, humming

to herself. It didn't take long. She came out in a blast of perfume with her face vivid with mascara, rouge, lipstick, and eyebrow pencil.

"Not bad for an old doll, eh?" She arched her brows at me.

"Not bad at all. But you should take a coat; it's cold out there."

She put on a pearl-grey imitation-fur jacket and a fluffy pink scarf and out we went.

My friend had a small law practice in an office he rented from a larger firm. He came out as soon as we arrived, and Rhonda had the expected effect on the receptionist and other staff as we filed into his office. The paperwork was done within an hour and I turned the money over to her.

"Maybe you should count it," I said.

"Nah, it would take too long, let's just get this over with."

On our way out, my conscience caught up with me. It didn't feel right to just cut her loose with all that cash. I tried to convince her to get the money into her bank and not walk around with it, especially to the places she was likely to go. She looked at me as if I were crazy. The thought of showing off with that wad—to feel like she was somebody, likely for the last time in her life—was too appealing. It was after lunch by now. I suggested we get something to eat, hoping it would put some sense into her head about the money.

I knew a couple of places near the law office I thought she might like and we walked to the nearest one. She took my arm and bumped her hip against me as we walked. I was about to tell her to straighten up when I noticed the fishy looks some of the sleek young downtown office types were giving us, so I pulled her closer. She hooted with delight, obviously enjoying herself and the spectacle we were making of ourselves. There was a booth open at the café. Rhonda ordered a beer while she looked at the menu. She ordered a hot hamburger sandwich, likely the last solid food she'd see for a while. She ate half her sandwich and picked daintily at her fries and gravy with her fingers. Giving me a defiant look, she ordered another beer. I worked on her about depositing the money, maybe taking out a thousand. A girl could feel pretty special with a grand in her purse, I told her. That did it. She agreed to go to her bank and I hustled her out before she changed her mind.

By the time we got to Rhonda's bank, it was about to close. She was showing the effects of the beers she'd had, and was having second thoughts about depositing the money. She couldn't make up her mind whether to be belligerent or provocative with me. While she was deciding, I managed to get her inside the bank just as one of the clerks reached the door with her bracelet of keys to lock up. The disapproving look on the clerk's face must have been enough for Rhonda to decide to stay belligerent. Cigarette jutting out of her raspberry lips, she swayed up to the nearest teller still at her post, ignoring the "next teller please" sign, and slapped her bag onto the counter. Squinting sideways at me and cursing, she rummaged around in her bag and pulled out the wad of money.

"Count it. I wanna make a deposit!" she snarled at the teller, a startled young Chinese girl.

An older woman with a tight perm and even tighter lips, likely the head teller, noticed the commotion and came over. She looked even more disapproving than the downtown office workers who saw us on the street. I edged over in case the situation got out of hand. The few customers still in the bank were glancing over at us like we were worms in their apple, and I noticed one of the staff members get up from her desk and scurry off, likely to find the manager. Rhonda and the head teller were hissing at each other like geese. The manager appeared. He seemed to know Rhonda, and from something in his eyes, I fathomed he found this rather amusing, especially the state his head teller had worked herself into. From what I could tell, this wasn't the first time Rhonda had made a nuisance of herself at that bank, but she was tolerated out of respect for Lou, who also had his account there. From the manager's patience with Rhonda, I gathered it must have been some account.

Very quickly the manager grasped the problem, solved it, calmed the head teller, then looked over at me. He gave me a dry "thank you" for seeing that the money was properly put away. In all the excitement, Rhonda had forgotten to take out the thousand dollars for herself, and I wasn't going to remind her. By then the money had been counted and deposited, the teller and head teller were gone, and Rhonda had calmed down. The manager led us to the door and let us out himself.

The bank manager's charm was still working on Rhonda back on the street. She beamed at me, took my arm, and suggested I drive her back to her place for another beer. There wasn't much temptation in that, but I didn't let it show. I kidded with her until an empty taxi came by. The driver heard my whistle and cut across traffic to pull up at the curb beside us. I opened the door for her.

"Hey!" she yelled in surprise. "I don't wanna lousy cab. I wanna go in your truck!"

"Come on," I said. "Dolled up like that, you don't belong in a truck. I'd get you a limo if I saw one. I'm gonna pay the driver to take you anywhere you want to go. And here, this is for you!" By now she was in the taxi. I put a hundred dollars in her hand.

"What's that fer?" she cried, "I didn't earn it! What'r you doin?"

"Well, you were going at that teller so bad you forgot to take the grand out of the bank for yourself. This should buy you a few drinks."

"Well, you sonnuvabitch! I shoulda never listened to ya. I knew it!"

I reached over and gave the driver a twenty. I knew she wasn't going far and that would more than cover the trip. When I turned back to face her, she was blinking away tears. She gave me a long hug and kiss, smearing that raspberry lipstick halfway across my face.

"Geez, Rhonda, what am I gonna tell my wife?"

"You bastard, tell 'er she's lucky I never got to earn that hundred!"

I drove down to Fishermen's Terminal before dawn the next morning, the scent of Rhonda's perfume still heavy in the truck. My new acquisition was tied right up to the float now with several grimy workboats rafted up alongside it. Mooring lines creaked as I stepped aboard. A bilge pump came on and spurted a stream of dirty water from a hull fitting onto the float where my foot had just been. The key Rhonda had given me wouldn't open the padlock on the cabin door at first, and I had to fiddle with it. Finally, it worked. I slid open the door and gingerly stepped down into the gloom of the cabin. As I waited for my eyes to adjust to the darkness, I felt the damp cold, and the mixed stench of wood rot, stove oil, garbage, and old cigarette smoke surrounded me until I was saturated. I edged over to the cold stove and pulled the window curtains open. It was just getting light outside, but the area lights on the float were still on, filling the cabin with a strange orange glow. The light seemed to be absorbed into the dark recesses of the cabin. The stovetop was the only surface that gave off a reflection—a testament to Rhonda's polishing.

The layout of the cabin was simple. The stove was on the starboard side by the door. Beside the stove was a countertop with cupboards underneath and a small sink in the middle. At its forward end was a seat, likely where Rhonda sat when she was aboard. On the port side was a narrow day bunk with drawers underneath that extended from the rear of the cabin to the helm. The helm seat was set up on a cabinet that housed a two-way bar refrigerator. There was a small compartment beside the door that contained a head. A narrow table was attached to its forward wall and extended out along the front of the day bunk. It was hinged so it could be swung up and out of the way, but judging from its load of darkening old newspapers and magazines, it hadn't been moved in years. The main bunk was under the foredeck. It had about three feet of headroom and was separated from the rest of the cabin by a stained curtain. It must have been where Rhonda and Lou slept together when she was aboard.

I stood there a good ten minutes looking around, but the cabin wasn't getting any brighter even though it was nearly full daylight outside. I opened the rest of the curtains. Some light came in, but the cabin stayed curiously dark. Looking closer at one of the windows, I noticed a brown tinge to the glass. I wiped at it with my knuckles and light flooded in through the trail I had left on the glass. On my knuckles was a damp brown residue that smelled, with sickening intensity, of stale tobacco smoke. Looking around for somewhere to wipe off my knuckles, I realized that the entire cabin and everything in it was covered in the same tobacco glaze. I left at that point, shutting the door behind me, and breathed in the sweet air outside. Once on the float, I got down and washed off my knuckles in the salt water then rubbed them on the rough timber structure to get rid of the stain, but I still felt clammy and contaminated.

Later that day, after a long hot shower at home, I went back inside the Rhonda wearing gloves, coveralls, and a dust mask to see if there was anything to salvage before putting it up for sale. There was plenty of stuff aboard: under the main bunk were four cases of canned soups along with two cases of wide-mouth mason jars with lids and rings ready for canning salmon. In the space above it were pillows and bedclothes; extra blankets; a gallon of cheap sherry; plastic garbage bags full of clothes, some men's but mostly women's; a cardboard box full of mildewed paperbacks; and an old portable radio. Under the day bunk were boxes of flashers, hoochies, spoons, and other trolling gear; half a bale of gillnet web; spare corks; and at least a dozen spools of hanging twine and mending twine. Stashed in crannies around the cabin were tobacco tins full of fittings for copper tubing; silicon bronze screws; galvanized nails; bolts and nuts of various sizes, many of them stainless steel; seal bombs; electrical components; and assortments of useless junk. An entire carburetor assembly for a three-hundred-cubic-inch Ford straight six, which turned out to be the *Rhonda's* engine, was wrapped in a rag and jammed in beside the pump toilet. There were pots, frying pans, dishes, cups, glasses, cutlery, and a case each of canned spaghetti and Kraft Dinner in the galley cupboards. It went on, this inventory of a man's life, none of which I wanted to salvage.

On the floor under the table where Lou must have spent a lot of his time sitting was a pair of felt slippers. At the edge of the table nearest the day bunk was a large roll-your-own cigarette machine. The black plastic handle was shiny from use and free of the brown glaze covering everything else in the cabin. I continued to rummage through the boat half-heartedly, but my eyes kept wandering to that cigarette machine and those felt slippers.

Rhonda must have been right about Lou's navigation skills because there were no electronics on board other than a small Ekolite sounder that looked too old to work. There was no radar or autopilot, and only one small VHF radio. A few old charts were rolled up and stuck into a corner by the helm seat. The only compass was a battered old Dirigo in its original wooden box, which had been cracked and distorted by many years of sun coming through the windshield. There was no relief to the grime and squalor.

The only items I found worth salvaging were a couple of decent hand tools and a small Finn knife. There may have been more, maybe even a cache of money aboard, but I was done raking through the remnants of that sad life.

I looked at his slippers again. They were the only attempt at comfort I could see. Maybe he put them on every time he came back after one of his walks. Rhonda had said that after he left her the last time, he kept calling to see if he could come over to visit. Most of the time she had company, so he would call back again and again to see if they had left. She said this had made her so angry she began saying there was someone with her even when there wasn't, and sometimes she just wouldn't answer the phone. The times he had been in a hurry to get up the float must have been to make those phone calls. Between walks, he likely sat at the table in his slippers, re-reading the old newspapers and magazines, and smoking or rolling himself more cigarettes until he couldn't stand it anymore and hurried up to the public telephone to make another call.

If there was any more to his life, it wasn't showing in that cabin. There were no chairs for visitors. Without friends, he didn't need any. He must have sat on his day bunk to use his cigarette machine. There wasn't a television set or radio for a little music or news. Not a bottle of whisky; not even a deck of cards. There was a coffee pot on the stove with a sinister-looking black syrup on the bottom and a few pounds of unopened Maxwell House in one of the cupboards, so he must have made coffee for himself. There were some rotting onions and potatoes in the cupboards. Maybe he had them when he got tired of his canned soups and spaghetti or Kraft Dinner. The bar fridge was empty, but it smelled of spoiled food. Maybe he kept eggs and some kind of meat in it at one time to cook with the onions and potatoes. He must have slept in the day bunk, with its filthy pillow and grey army blankets. There was no light to read by. In one of the drawers under the bunk was a change of underwear and a plaid shirt. The pants he wore must have been the only ones he owned. In a little cupboard above the sink was an old-fashioned razor, shaving soap in a cup, an old comb, and a bar of orange soap. Other than that, there were no other personal items aboard. The medals Rhonda had mentioned weren't there, nor were any letters, photographs, or birthday or Christmas cards. There were no pocketknives or watches, no keepsakes or souvenirs of a trip somewhere. He might have left some of these things with Rhonda, but she wasn't the kind of person to look after them. She didn't even look capable of looking after her own personal items, except maybe the sombrero.

I found myself wondering how a lifetime could culminate in so little. Even his boat was gone now, sold cheap by an ex-common-law wife who didn't want him around. Rhonda said that he wanted her to put an ad in the paper to sell the boat as soon as they got back to Vancouver. Sell it fast, he'd said. Of course, she'd had other things to do and didn't get around to it before I appeared on her doorstep, or more precisely, in her bedroom. Maybe getting rid of the boat before he died was Lou's final act in an ongoing rejection of normal life that started the day he realized Rhonda would never change. Maybe ending up with no friends and neglecting his boat the way he did was part of that. But even so, hopeless as it was, he kept trying to reach her. He had looked out for her, paid the rent on her suite, and kept calling her even as she kept brushing him off.

After he died, all that would be left was his money. The bank manager must have known what he wanted done with it. From the patience he'd shown Rhonda, chances were she was the beneficiary. Lou didn't seem to have any friends to speak of; Rhonda didn't mention any relatives, and he didn't appear the type to leave his money to a worthy cause. He had already given Rhonda his power of attorney; all there was left to do was leave her the money. The only question was whether she'd get it in a monthly draw, or all at once. If the arrangement was to dole it out to her, she'd live longer. If she got it all at once, it would kill her. More than likely she'd get monthly draws. That way he could look out for her longer.

Getting back into the fresh air had never felt so good. It was nearly dark by now, which surprised me. I locked the door and got out of my protective gear on the aft deck. With the salvaged knife and tools rolled into a tight bundle in my coveralls, I stepped off the Rhonda and onto the float for what I hoped would be the last time. The boat listed with my weight on the rail and the bilge pump came on, again just missing my boot. It almost felt like a summer night as I walked up the float to the ramp leading to the parking lot. The tide was up and the ramp was nearly level. There was a garbage container close to where I'd parked my truck. I thought of tossing my bundle into it; there wasn't much in it worth keeping. But looking around at the city, alive with noises and smells, its lights reflecting in the water, I didn't. They were something to remember him by, and Lou deserved at least that. I put them in the truck and started for home.

"Funny," I said to Valerie as we sat down to a late supper, "how one man's tragedy can turn into another man's luck."

"Well, at least his licence will live on and be turned into something good on our new boat," she said, understanding me as usual.

"Yeah, I still remember how the *T.K.* turned out. I knew I shouldn't have sold it to that hippie."

"So you don't want the same thing to happen to the *Rhonda?*"

"No, but I'm sure as hell not keeping it. And nobody in their right mind would buy it."

"Well, as you keep telling me, the world is full of idiots, so you never know," she said. "Besides, you've done what you had to do about the licence. The *Rhonda* is really just a loose end now."

"Some loose end."

"Never mind. Something will turn up. Let's go to bed. I don't think I can smell Rhonda's perfume off you anymore."

12

||| THE LOOSE END |||

The day after I'd bought the Rhonda, Otto called the house and left a message with Valerie saying I needed to call him about something important. When I returned his call later that evening, he told me he had just heard from someone that length measurement for licence transfers had changed. Owners were no longer involved. The measurement was now done by two fisheries officers, and to the inch. As a result, new boats that were too long for the licences being transferred to them were having their bows cut back to match the exact length of the licences. Brutal as it was, that was all some of the owners could do, faced with lost fishing time and extra expense if they started looking for a larger licence.

The chance of that happening with the Rhonda's licence certainly caught my attention. The next morning I checked and found my measurement had been right. I needed to make up one foot and four inches in length. My chance of brazening it through was gone. I had to use a loophole I'd found out about when selling the *T.K.*

Under the Fisheries Department system, the size of boats for licence transfer purposes was based on overall length. The loophole was that a vessel's size in tonnage could also be used. This had to be determined under the rules of the British Registry of Shipping, which still applied in Canada at the time, provided the vessel was listed in the registry. The tonnage had to be calculated by a marine surveyor. I'd found a reasonably creative surveyor could use this system to calculate that two boats of somewhat different lengths were the same tonnage under the registry's rules. In the eyes of the Fisheries Department, this made them the same size, and licence transfers between the two vessels were automatically approved. I had the marine surveyor I'd used when selling the *T.K.* down at the *Rhonda* the next day. He was familiar with the Deltaga hulls and after measuring the *Rhonda*, he assured me he could make the tonnages for the two boats come out the same.

A complication arose in getting the *Rhonda* listed in the British Registry of Shipping because another vessel with the same name was already listed. The *Rhonda*'s name had to be changed. *Rhonda XXX* was tempting as it better fit her namesake, but I went with *Rhonda X* because it was less work. It took an afternoon to make sure the registry requirements were met: painting the new name and port of registry on the stern and the new name on the bows, and carving the official number into the main beam. With everything done, the marine surveyor checked my work and approved it, promising to get his certification into the Ships Registry the following day. After seeing him off, I put a "for sale" sign in the *Rhonda*'s window, thinking of ways to celebrate this milestone with Valerie that evening.

But just as she and I were sitting down to dinner, the telephone rang. Ignoring my first impulse, I answered it.

"You the guy sellin the boat?" a voice bellowed. "An' yer gonna hafta speak up; my hearin aid's busted!"

I was selling a boat, but this didn't sound like a buyer. More likely it was one of my friends at the False Creek Fishermen's Terminal joking around.

"Okay, who is this?" I asked.

"What's that? Can't hear ya! Speak up, dammit," the voice roared at me.

"Who is this?" I shouted.

"This is Lyall. Lyall Crawford. You know me!"

The voice did sound familiar. In fact, I had just heard it as I was leaving the False Creek Fishermen's Terminal after seeing off the marine surveyor. It had come from inside a garbage dumpster on the edge of the parking lot. As I was passing by, the voice had yelled "heads up" just as a sprocket and shaft that looked like part of a drum drive flew out of the dumpster, narrowly missing my head. I picked it up and walloped the side of the dumpster with it, making a clang that reverberated across the harbour. It caused a string of curses and threats and a few pieces of wood and scrap metal to follow the shaft out of the dumpster. I laughed and drove home.

"Oh yeah! You're the guy in the dumpster! What do you want with my boat?"

"What? What? Speak up, dammit."

"I said, you're the guy in the dumpster." By now Valerie had come over to see why I was shouting.

"So, you the guy that bashed the dumpster with that shaft? My ears are still ringin! Maybe that's what blew out my hearin aid, haw haw!" He laughed as though he thought it was a great joke.

Once I heard that laugh, I placed him. He was one of the regular scavengers who rode around on a bicycle hung with shopping bags checking out the dumpsters along the seawall at the False Creek Terminal. Fat and raucous, he reminded me of the big seagull you find in every flock that tries to chase the others away from food so he can eat it himself.

"So whadaya want with the R*honda*?" I yelled.

"Well, I wanna buy 'er, sonny. I seen yer sign on 'er."

"What are you talking about?"

"Yer sellin an I'm buyin, simple as that."

"Wait a minute. You've got to have the money first."

"I got the money."

"Do you even know how much I'm asking?"

"Naw, but I got enough!"

"Six thousand bucks." I was actually going to ask five thousand, not expecting to get it. I was just hoping to put Lyall off with the higher price.

"No problem, I got enough."

"From dumpster diving?"

"Hell no. I just do that for fun. I got a pension. Besides, I still got money from my prize fightin days."

"You were a prize fighter?"

"That's right, sonny. I was the bare-knuckle brawlin champeen of Britannia Beach. Retired undefeated in '54."

There were more odd characters lurking around the waterfront than anywhere else in Vancouver. Among this crew, a dumpster-diving, ex-bare-knuckle brawling "champeen" of Britannia Beach didn't stand out so much as fit right in. It just made him a bigger nut on the same tree. From what I'd seen though, some of those nuts had money and maybe my caller was one of them. It was enough to keep me interested, but not enough to keep me shouting into the phone.

"Tell you what, if you're that interested, and you got the money, I'll be down there in the morning."

"I'm outta town tomorrow. I gotta see her tonight!"

"Look, it's dark and you can't see much tonight. Come down after you get back to town. I'm going to eat my dinner now."

"But you might sell 'er before I get back to town. Why not finish supper and meet me down there in a couple of hours? It won't even be ten yet, okay? Okay?"

I finally agreed—only to stop his wheedling.

It was well before ten when I got to the False Creek Fishermen's Terminal, driven more by curiosity than the expectation of a sale. Down at the float where the Rhonda was tied up, I could see a figure standing under one of the area lights. The closer I got, the bigger he looked: a huge belly hanging over stained khaki pants held up by belt and suspenders, fishermen's romeos, a red-checked logger's shirt, and a Black Watch cap perched on a head the size of a medium pumpkin. As I got up to him, he reached out a hand the size of a catcher's mitt for a handshake. He was grinning from ear to ear and the orange glow of the lamp he was standing under gave him the look of a happy Jack-o-lantern.

"Lyall's the name," he said. "Sorry to drag ya away from the missus. Good-lookin woman. Can't blame ya for wantin ta stay home."

"What the hell? So how do you know my wife?"

"No offence, no offence. I just seen ya come down ta yer boat tagether. I seen the ring on her finger. Figured ya was smart enough to marry 'er so as not ta risk losin 'er to a handsome devil like me, haw haw."

I didn't answer, but my first impression of him as a yokel was gone: his two unblinking little eyes, half-hidden in the folds of his creased face, were inspecting me as closely as I was inspecting him. He was already working me like a born huckster. It did look like he'd been in the fight game, though. Up close, his head and face showed more scars than Johnny Bower's, the old-time NHL goalie who played without a mask. One of his ears was cauliflowered, and the other drooped as if it had been partly torn off at some point. Handsome he certainly wasn't, but he was persuasive enough to get me out of a promising evening with my wife onto this wild goose chase.

I climbed aboard to unlock the door so he could have a look inside. Luckily I was braced when he came over the rail. The Rhonda rolled like a pig; the mooring lines screeched and both pumps came on to spray bilge water over the float timbers. Something in the cabin hit the floor with a crash.

"Well, she's lively. I allus liked a lively boat," he laughed, showing surprising balance for a man his size.

I got the door unlocked and slid it open. He barged into the cabin like a bear into a blueberry patch before I could get in to check what had crashed to the floor. It didn't sound like any glass had broken, so I left it and stepped down onto the float leaving him to root around inside the cabin.

A Float was deserted at that time of night. Traffic sounds from the city were faint and far away. Water lapped softly at the float timbers, signalling that the tide was changing. I had an early morning coming up and would have already been in bed with Valerie if not for Lyall. Worse yet, he didn't look anywhere near having the money to come up with the price. I wondered what Lyall saw in the Rhonda. Maybe he thought there was money stashed aboard by Lou. Now that everything was set for the licence transfer, all I wanted to do was get rid of that sad mess of a boat.

There wasn't a sound coming out of the Rhonda now, which I took to be a bad sign. Climbing aboard, I peered into the cabin. The stuff that had been on the main bunk was piled on the floor. There was a light on behind the bulkhead, giving a soft glow to the bunk space and making it look almost cozy. Lyall was lying on his back with his arms folded behind his head, propped up against the spare bedding in the bow of the boat. He looked out at me contentedly over his size twelve romeos.

"I'll take 'er!" he roared.

"What? You sure?" I replied. "Would you like to start the engine at least?"

"What fer? I know it runs good. I know the boat. Hell, I even useta know the broad she's named fer."

"You knew Rhonda?"

"That's what I said, bub."

"How'd you know her?"

He raised his head and gave me a look, not believing I'd be naive enough to ask that, and didn't answer.

"Forget I asked. So you've decided?"

"Yup. She's perfect."

"Okay, we've got a deal then."

"Only yer askin too much."

"Whadaya mean too much? I thought you already agreed to the price."

"No, I didn't. I was just negotiatin with ya."

"Geez, I was just getting to like you, Lyall, and now you turn out to be a piker." I meant it as a joke.

"Who you callin a piker?" he bellowed, starting up.

Lyall had forgotten the low headroom in the bunk. He cracked his head against the ceiling and fell back. That infuriated him and he spat out a string of blasphemy.

I looked around for something to defend myself with. A sawed-off shotgun would have been good, but the best I found was a cast iron skillet on the stove. By now Lyall had managed to get out of the bunk and stand up. There was something like six feet between us. He snarled and started to close in.

I got ready to swing the skillet, making him laugh. "My old girlfriend used to swing one a them at me. Too bad she wasn't much of a cook, haw haw!"

I had to laugh as well. Putting the skillet back on the stove warily, I felt like I'd just avoided tangling with an angry bear in his cage.

"So, you got a problem with the price?" I asked.

"Yep. Five thousant is what I'll pay. Not a penny more!"

"Okay, you got a deal." I wasn't going to haggle if he was offering more than I had originally expected.

He stepped toward me and we shook hands. His smell reminded me of an old trapper: equal parts wood smoke, stale sweat, stomach acid, and woollen clothing. It overpowered the cabin odour, as if already taking over the Rhonda from Lou. I asked him for a deposit.

"What?" he roared.

"A deposit to hold 'er in case I get another offer," I said reasonably.

"What the hell smartass stunt you pullin' at me, sonny? You don't trust me?" He looked like he was ready to take a swing at me. I looked for the frying pan.

"It's normal business, Lyall. You mean to say you came without anything to leave as a deposit?"

"I never bought a boat before." My reasonable tone seemed to be calming him down. He plunged a hand into his pocket and came out with some crumpled bills. He held them up, squinted at them, and thrust them at me. "Here. It's all I got. Twenty dollars."

His anger was gone. He was looking worried that I'd turn him down.

"All right, Lyall. For you, I'll do this." I had a small pad and pen in my pocket, and wrote out a receipt. "When can you get the rest?"

"For sure by Satiday," he said. "Good and early."

Highly doubting that it would happen, I said, "That'll be fine, but if you don't have the money by Saturday, there'll be an ad in the paper on Monday." We locked the boat and walked up the float together.

"So, you were the bare-knuckle brawling champion of Britannia Beach you say?"

"Yup, I do say. Toughest sonnuvabitch up there. Useta prove it every Satiday night." We were halfway up the ramp from the float to the parking lot, and he was already wheezing. "Course I was younger then."

"I guess. And you did this for money?"

"Damn right! Better than workin in that mine! Made five hunnert bucks for a couple a them fights!"

"Not bad. Where did you fight?"

"In th' back a' the rec hall mostly. I had a few in the hotel parkin lot, but that wasn't fer money, jist fer fun. Th' rec hall was run by an ol' Italian fella. He was the ref an' his brother was kinda my manager. Them miners loved it. There was a lotta bettin, mostly on how long it would take me ta get a knockout."

"And you never lost?"

"Never. Gotta admit I came close once or twice though. Somma them was real wars, ya know. Them Italians brought in ringers from th' States, negra fellas, a coupla times. But I had this technique, see. I'd move in close an' step on their toes so they couldn' back away, an' hammer 'em in th' gut! Easier on th' hands than punchin em in the head! Them guys was trained boxers, but they never knew how t' deal with my technique, haw haw."

"So, when did you give it up? In '54 you said?"

"Hey, hey, it's not like I gave up! I just stopped when I was good an' ready. Yup, that was nineteen an' fifty-four. Bought me a bran' new '54 Ford convertible. Powder blue. Got me any girl I wanted! I coulda gone on another ten years, but I didn' wanna ruin my good looks, haw haw."

We had reached his bicycle by now. For once there were no shopping bags full of dumpster loot in the carrier or hanging off the handlebars. He got some pant clips out of his pocket, carefully clamped his pant cuffs around his ankles, and lined the bicycle up in the direction he was going. He swung aboard, and turned back to me.

"So, we got a deal?" he yelled even though I was standing right beside him. "So, five thousand cash, Satiday mornin' early?"

"Yep, I'll be here."

"Good, but ya know what?"

"What?"

"Fer a young buck, ya sure ain't much at negotiatin. Ya was robbed! I woulda gone ta six grand if youda stuck t'yer guns! I just made a thousand bucks off ya, sonny, haw haw."

With that he pedalled off into the night, not a light showing on his bicycle, a man in control of his universe.

⁞⁞⁞⁞⁞

The next Saturday I was down at the harbour before seven. The weather was good: dry and not too cold. The only person moving on the floats was one of the old live-aboard fishermen, heading up to the washrooms with a towel around his neck and his toilet kit in his hand. He lived on a gorgeous old wooden tuna boat that he had converted to a troller after the war. He had a house, but after his wife died, he rented it out and moved onto his boat. It was rumoured he had a lot of money. The story may have started because he fished the boat without a deckhand, which was rare for a troller with a large boat like his, especially for someone his age. We waved at each other and smiled. I poured coffee out of my thermos and drank it leaning over the wharf handrail and looking out over the fleet. Normally I would have gone straight down to the *Ruby Dawn*, but this time, wondering if Lyall would show up, I hung around the wharf area until my coffee was gone. Daylight had slowly taken over from the orange area lamps in the parking lot and on the floats until they finally blinked out. Lyall still hadn't arrived. I waited another few minutes, then began to walk down to my boat, thinking that the sale was too good to be true after all.

I had been aboard for less than an hour when I heard a heavy slap on the hull and Lyall's bellow.

"Hullo, the boat! You in there, kid?"

He was on the finger float grinning up at me. There were about a half dozen good teeth left in his mouth and he was showing them all in his obvious joy.

"Sorry I'm late, kid. Didn't have enough cash at home. Hadda go ta my special bank because I knew ya was too smart t'take my cheque. Haw haw!"

He handed me up a crumpled McDonalds bag that looked like it came from a dumpster.

"Better count 'er," he shouted. "But don't take long; I'm itchin t'move in!"

The bag held exactly five thousand dollars, in tens, twenties, and hundreds. Some of the bills were fairly new, but most were crumpled and worn. Some of them smelled like coffee, as if they'd been stored in a coffee can buried somewhere.

"Looks good, Lyall. Now we got some paperwork to do."

"Ta hell with th' paperwork! Just throw me them keys!"

Not quite trusting his hand-eye coordination, I handed them to him, and he lumbered off. Soon he was hauling shopping bags full of what I assumed to be his belongings down to the Rhonda.

It didn't take long for my neighbours on the dock to realize what was happening. A couple of them came over to let me know they weren't happy. They said Lyall was noisy, messy, and insulting, and they suspected he would steal anything that wasn't nailed down on their boats. Worst of all, he wasn't a fisherman. I assured them that he would be moving to D Float where the unlicensed boats were tied up. Their retort was that Lyall was too devious for them to believe that. The end of the dock where the Rhonda was moored was already a slum, they told me, and it would be ten times worse with him there. It wasn't until I promised to personally go over in the morning to make sure Lyall moved the Rhonda that they went back to their boats, still shaking their heads and muttering to themselves.

Early next morning, I went to see Lyall. Even from a distance I could see why my neighbours were upset. The Rhonda had become a garbage scow overnight. Piles of what must have been Lou's things were thrown out onto its decks and the adjacent dock. The rain that had begun overnight did nothing to dull the stench rising from the mess. Soaked cardboard boxes lay collapsing among dark mounds of old blankets, dirty bedding, and green garbage bags. Rats had already started work in a few places, and it wouldn't be long before the seagulls moved in.

There was smoke coming out of the chimney and a whiff of good coffee threading through the reek of the garbage. I slapped the Rhonda's hull, told Lyall I was coming aboard, and got a growl in return. The coffee smell was stronger in the cabin, sparring with the leftover smells of tobacco smoke and PineSol, which Lyall must have been cleaning with. Much of the brown film had been wiped away, exposing the original cream-coloured paintwork. A couple of windows had been opened and the stove gleamed with fresh polish. The table was cleared off and a coal oil lamp still burned there. Lyall stood by the sink with his pant legs rolled up and grey Stanfield's underwear top unbuttoned, a large wet rag in his hand, not looking happy to see me.

"Ya know, I already chased that little peckerhead of a wharfinger away with a warnin not ta come back. Do I gotta do the same with you?" It was the first time I'd heard him speak in a normal volume.

"Good morning to you too, Lyall. Sounds like you got your hearing aid fixed, eh?"

"Yeah, but don't change the subject. I know why you're here. You damn fishermen don't think I'm good enough fer this lousy dock an' want me out."

"Hey, listen, I already told you that you'd have to move, and you said you would. That's all the peckerhead wharfinger was trying to tell you. And you sure as hell gotta get rid of that garbage out there."

"Well, I'll move it when I'm damn good an' ready. An' not before, an' not because a' some damn rules about licences an' stuff, anyway. Besides, I'm still housecleanin, as ya can plainly see."

He looked like he was having trouble staying angry. Either the *Rhonda* was having a good effect on his disposition or he knew how funny he looked standing there with his pant legs rolled up. I looked around the cabin some more and didn't say anything.

"So, you wanna have a coffee or what? I was just gonna have some," he said.

He got two cups out, put them on the table, and then reached over to the stove for the coffee pot. It was a fancy one, made in Italy. It looked like it might get crushed in Lyall's big paw.

"Neat coffee pot, Lyall, where'd you get it?" I was going to ask if he'd found it in a dumpster somewhere but resisted.

"Oh, a friend gave it to me. Why?"

"No reason. You just don't see many around like it. Made in Italy, I see."

"Yup."

His fingers were too thick to get around the handle properly. He held it delicately between his thumb and fingertips, reminding me of a conductor holding a baton. He poured, and the coffee came out in a thin stream, dark and strong-smelling.

"Same friend give you the coffee?" I asked.

"Yeah, as a matter of fact. So?"

"Nothing. It just smells great. I bet it isn't Maxwell House."

"It ain't. Ya want anything in it?" he growled.

"Cream and sugar if you got it."

"Yeah, I figured so," he sneered. "I drink mine black."

He produced a half-sized can of Pacific evaporated milk and a box of sugar cubes from the drawer where Lou had kept broken hand tools and assorted nuts and bolts.

"Well, ya might as well siddown," he said.

Being too thick to slide behind the table, he planted himself at the end of it on the day bunk instead. There was a chrome kitchen chair aboard now. I pulled it over beside the table and sat down. Lyall reached back and pulled a bottle of Hudson's Bay rum out from under a new cushion on the day bunk. He put it on the table with a thump.

"These days I keep my drinkin down, ya know, but today I'm celebratin. Call it a housewarmin." He poured a good shot into both our cups, filling them to the brim.

"Well, here's to a long, happy live-aboard, Lyall," I said, and we clicked our cups together without spilling much.

It was good coffee, and held its own against the rum. We finished our first cup without saying a lot and then he poured us another. His cantankerous nature was mellowing fast as the rum did its work. I took advantage of that to bring his attention to the paperwork still needing to be signed to transfer the *Rhonda* over to him.

"It was what you agreed to, remember?" I said. "I had to get the *Rhonda* into the Ships Registry to transfer her licence onto my new boat without the risk of getting screwed over the size of it by fisheries. The good part for you is that your boat will be listed in the British Registry of Shipping."

"Yeah, yeah. Well, if ya ever need help fightin them fisheries bastards, let me know. I got a friend in Ottawa," he said, deadpan.

"What's that?"

"A very good friend a' mine is big in Ottawa."

"That's what I thought you said."

"Ever heard a' Judy LaMarsh?"

"Sure, everybody's heard of her."

"Well, she's my girlfriend, ya know."

"What?"

"Yep, ya heard right. In fact, I'm thinkin a' phonin her up today about that peckerhead of a wharfinger tryin t'give me a hard time!"

"Judy LaMarsh. Of Ottawa. Okay, where do you know her from?"

"Met her right here in Vancouver."

"So if she's the Judy LaMarsh that's the Minister of something in Ottawa, how did you meet her in Vancouver?"

"She came out fer a radio talk show or somethin. I don't remember now, it's been a few years ago. Anyhow, I phoned her up. She said I sounded interestin. Salt of the earth type an' all that. Wouldn' mind meetin me."

"She told you all that on the radio?"

"Jeez, yer dense sometimes, kid. Off the air a' course. We were talkin like that durin a commercial."

"I don't believe this, Lyall."

"Ya don't? Lissen, I never lie, not about this kinda stuff anyway. Have a look at this then, smartass." He pulled a fat wallet out of his hip pocket, took out a business card without having to dig around for it, and handed it to me. Sure enough, it said Judy LaMarsh, Member of Parliament.

"Look at the back now."

"Lyall," it said, "call me anytime. XX Judy." There was a number and *private line* was underlined.

"How's them fer apples, eh? An' see them Xs? They mean kisses, in case ya didn' know."

I shook my head in amazement and handed back the card.

"So how did you meet her again?"

"Like I said, on the radio."

"No, I mean physically, like face to face."

"I went to her hotel room."

"What! How'd you do that?"

"Easy. I went to the radio station she was at; watched her come out an' followed her taxi."

"How? Did you have a car?"

"Naw, on my bike."

"On your bike? Come on!"

"Wal, it wasn't that far, only ta th' Hotel Vancouver. An' traffic was bad that day. Wasn't hard, anyways."

"And they let you into the hotel?"

"Sure, why not? I was dressed good. Had more teeth then too. I even bought her some flowers in that little gift shop they have in the lobby."

"I don't believe this!"

"Why not? Ya think only you guys that talk good get the girls? Ya don' know the half of it, sonny."

"How'd you find out what room she was in?"

"Bellhop's my nephew. He took me up in the elevator an' tol' me where to find her room."

"Did he think it was funny?"

"Funny? Hell no! Why should he? Lissen, sonny, ya don' seemta unnerstan' I useta be a ladies' man."

"I thought you were the bare-knuckle brawling champ."

"I was that too. Ya wouldn' believe how wimmin liked ta tend ta my cuts an' bruises. Course, I met Judy after my fightin days was over. But still good-lookin. Got t' admit I let myself go a bit lately, though."

"So how did you get into her room? Your nephew the bellhop?"

"Naw. He cut an' run after I got outta the elevator. I found her room, knocked on the door, an' said 'Flowers from an admirer.'"

"And she let you in?"

"Not at first. I hadda explain I was the 'salt a' the earth' guy she'd talked to on the radio. She kinda thought about it, but she let me in."

"Well, what happened then?"

"That's none a' yer business. I will say she made us drinks outta the mini bar thing, though. First time I seen one."

"Did you see her again?"

"Course I seen her again! Course I did. Many times. She useta fly out here t' see me just fer a change from that Ottawa bunch, I figure. Hey, she almost had me comin out t' Ottawa one time just t' punch out that bastard Trudeau. Didn' know if she was kiddin or not, but it fell through. She useta kid a lot. She musta patched it up with Trudeau, but she never liked him much at all. Ya shoulda heard the names she called 'im. But that was only after she'd been drinkin a bit. Most a' the time she was a perfect lady. That was why I liked her so much. Had a raspy tongue in her head, though; just get her goin after a few drinks. I think she gave some Ottawa guy a black eye one time. That was the other reason I liked her so much: she had jam. Real jam. An' she wasn't tight. Didn' mind spendin a buck or two. Say, ya ever heard a' room service? Ya have? Wal, many a time we had room service, an' good stuff too. Steaks an' like that. I could still chew pretty good them days. Could chew an' talk at the same time. She useta love my stories. That was another reason I liked 'er: she was a good listener, fer a broad. Ya want more coffee, or ya okay with more rum?"

I put my hand over my cup. Lyall absentmindedly splashed a slug of rum into his own cup and continued his story.

"An' she useta call me all the time when she was in Ottawa, an' it wasn't always just ta tell me how much she missed me either. She wanted ta know what I thought about different things that were goin on, my opinion like. I was never shy a' tellin her what I thought. Sometimes I didn' even know what in hell she was talkin about but I gave her my opinion anyway."

He stopped talking and sat looking off into the distance. Careful not to break the spell, I took the bill of sale and Registry of Shipping transfer papers out of my jacket pocket and put them on the table. While his mind was still on Judy, I handed him a pen and pointed to each place he had to sign. Surprisingly, he did it without hesitation, like a trusting child.

"Too bad she never got ta be prime minister," he went on after handing me back the pen. "I'd a' liked ta seen that. First thing I'da told her would be ta take that French off them cereal boxes. I guess them papers I signed were ta put the boat in my name, right? Okay, I figgered so.

"She talked about it, ya know. I mean about bein prime minister. Not much though, because she knew she didn' have much of a chance... Yeah, too bad she never got in or I mighta had a say in how this country was run, haw haw. Say, I cut out some stuff about her in th' newspapers. Wanta see 'em?"

Looking a little drunk, he heaved himself up from the day bunk and over to a pile of shopping bags of stuff he still hadn't put away. I got up too, disgusted with myself for being so wrapped up in his outrageous story that I'd missed my chance of getting him to move the Rhonda as I'd promised my neighbours. What really burned was that I had almost believed him. I told Lyall I had a lot to do that day and would be back to look at the clippings later. What I meant was I'd be back to make sure, one way or another, that he moved the boat. Pawing through the bags, he nodded without turning around.

It was nearly ten when I got back to the Ruby Dawn. More than two hours had gone by, and the work I had lined up to do that morning wasn't done. It left me out of sorts, the way I felt after wasting an evening watching television. To make it worse, the wharfinger stopped by. He was an easy going ex-postman who feared neither dog nor man, but he had met his match in Lyall. The wharfinger couldn't quite hide his satisfaction when telling me that, as far as the head wharfinger was concerned, the Rhonda was still mine. Until they saw the Ships Registry Blue Book showing it properly registered in Lyall's name, I was responsible for the boat. That meant I had to clean up Lyall's garbage if I couldn't get him to do it. And one way or another, the Rhonda had to move to D Dock that day. The bill of sale I showed him with Lyall's and my signatures didn't change things. I might like to know, he added, that the head wharfinger knew all about Lyall and thought it was a serious lapse in judgment on my part to have sold him the boat. If things weren't put right that very day, my moorage at a finger float, a spot coveted by many, might be short-lived.

At noon I ate the lunch Valerie had sent with me. She had made a great sandwich, as thick as the Vancouver phonebook and nearly as big across, but I hardly tasted it. After finishing, I headed out to take on Lyall again. As I came closer, I thought I heard snoring. I went aboard and slid open the door. He was sprawled out on the main bunk snoring like a grampus. The rum bottle stood on the table with less than a good shot remaining. It had been full when he had put it on the table earlier that morning. I went over to give him a shake. He was smiling, as if dreaming about something good, maybe Judy. It would have been churlish to wake him out of something so pleasant. Besides, I had just thought of another way to do what I needed to. It depended on him staying asleep a while longer. From the look of him, it was a good bet. I quietly closed his door and started back to the Ruby Dawn.

Pete happened to be walking down the dock just then. He was on his way to check his boat and smoke a cigar where his wife wouldn't complain about it. This was the first time he'd come down to his boat in a week and he didn't know what I had gotten myself into. Pete had an odd sense of humour. He started to laugh before I was done telling him about what had happened. When I told him what I had planned for Lyall, he laughed even harder and jumped at a chance to help.

Pete helped cast off the *Ruby Dawn* and we idled over to where the *Rhonda* was moored at the end of the dock. We quietly untied the workboat lying beside it and moved it alongside the boat ahead. While Pete tied up the workboat, I dropped some bumpers to protect the *Ruby Dawn's* clean white hull and gently nudged it up against the garbage-laden *Rhonda*. Using the bow, spring, and stern lines, we rafted the two boats together tightly. Pete untied the *Rhonda* from the dock, unplugged its power cord, and shoved us off. Once clear, I put the *Ruby Dawn* in gear and idled the two boats toward D Dock. Pete had gone ahead to find the easiest spot to moor the *Rhonda* and was waiting as we approached. Luckily there was room right up alongside the float about halfway to the end. By now it was raining harder, and the float was deserted.

With the two boats still tightly rafted together, I jockeyed the *Rhonda* in alongside the dock and Pete tied it up. When all was secure, I checked on Lyall. The smile had gone from his face and his snoring was quieter, but he slept on like a hibernating bear. I left his door open an inch or two, then Pete and I untied the *Ruby Dawn* and we headed back to A Dock.

"What a caper!" Pete laughed as we got underway. "Old Lyall'll swear off drinkin for sure when he wakes up and can't figure out how he got here!" We both had a good laugh as we imagined his befuddlement.

Ninety minutes after it all began, we had the *Ruby Dawn* moored as if nothing had happened. We went over to Pete's boat to dry off and have coffee since my galley was now empty, while his was well stocked as usual. Pete had remembered to start his oil stove before leaving to help out with Lyall and his boat was already warm when we got there. His coffee wasn't as good as Lyall's, and he poured rye into it rather than rum, but it warmed us up and chased away my foul mood of the morning. We sat looking out at the rain without saying much and soon I heard Pete begin to snore. He was still holding his cigar but it had gone out. I put it in the ashtray and let myself out of the cabin. There was still the remainder of Lyall's garbage to clean up.

Getting my rain gear and some plastic waste bags from the *Ruby Dawn*, I walked down to where the *Rhonda* had been moored. A Float was as deserted as D Float had been, and the afternoon was dimming fast. As I got to the piles of garbage, the lights along the dock clicked on and I thought I saw a rat scurry underneath it. Everything was soaked, much of it shredded, and I had to re-bag most of it before toting it up to the dumpster. It began to rain still harder as I worked, but even that wasn't enough to wash away the stench or the odd greasy spots the mess had left on the wooden deck.

When the last of it was in the dumpster, I checked on Pete. Awake from his nap, he had his cigar going again. He had made fresh coffee and gave me another cup spiked with his rye. We talked for a bit longer since I wouldn't be seeing him again for a while, busy as I was with the new boat I was building. It was early evening and still raining hard when we locked up our boats and walked to the parking lot together. I saw him off and stopped in at the wharfinger's office on the way to my truck. The office staff had gone for the day, but the wharfinger who had spoken to me that morning was still there. He said they were happy to see the *Rhonda* moved and the garbage on the float cleaned up. As far as they were concerned, what was left aboard the *Rhonda* could stay there until they heard complaints. He didn't expect many because the skippers tied up near Lyall weren't as fussy as the ones on A Float. With that, I headed for home.

Starting the next day, I worked long hours on the new boat and didn't get back down to the harbour until one morning several weeks later. After checking on the *Ruby Dawn*, I thought I'd look up Lyall to see how he'd survived the trip over from A Float and what he'd done about the garbage left aboard the *Rhonda*. I found a big padlock on the door, garbage all gone, and the decks washed down. As there was no one around to ask if they knew where Lyall might be, I stopped in at the wharfinger's office. They knew all right, and the head wharfinger called me into her office to tell me about it herself.

She crisply told me they'd pieced together that on the day Pete and I had moved him, Lyall had lain passed out on his bunk until the evening. He must have woken up with a terrible hangover and a head so thick that he didn't realize that the boats, people, and sounds around him were now different. He was so befuddled that he turned the wrong way when he went out the cabin door. Stepping over the rail expecting to land on timber decking, he found only cold black water.

He couldn't swim very well, and was freezing numb within minutes. There were tires hanging off the *Rhonda* as bumpers, but he was too heavy to use them to climb back aboard. His splashing and bellowing was heard by three deckhands, who were playing cards and drinking aboard a dragger moored nearby. Lyall was already near exhaustion when they came out to investigate. They had flashlights but it took them a while to find him since he had gone quiet and was shielded from their sight by the boats tied up along the float. By the time they spotted him he was barely moving. One of the deckhands jumped up onto the *Rhonda*'s bow, grabbed a pike pole, and hooked Lyall by the collar of his jacket to keep him from sinking. He guided Lyall over to the float where his buddies tried to pull him out by his arms, but the oily water had made him slippery and he kept sliding out of their grip. The deckhand with the pike pole then jumped down onto the float and, in a desperate final effort, hooked the pike pole in the seat of Lyall's pants and heaved along with the others. They finally dragged him up onto the dock where he lay like a dead walrus. One of them ran back to the dragger to call for help. That was when they noticed the blood on his pants where the pike pole had hooked his rump. The blood had already started pooling under him.

Lyall then groaned and started to shiver. He threw up. They rolled him onto his side so he wouldn't choke on his vomit and piled covers on him that they'd found in the Rhonda. He stopped groaning but his shivering got worse, to the point that water along the edges of the dock was rippling. Finally a siren was heard, first in the distance, then closer, and at last the lights of an ambulance appeared at the head of the ramp. Luckily the tide was up, making the ramp nearly level for the medics rushing down with their equipment. Attracted by the siren and flashing lights, a few people gathered along the railing at the edge of the wharf, and others came down onto the dock. The medics set up a work light and cut away Lyall's pants, exposing a jagged rent in his buttock that had caused the bleeding. His flesh had turned deathly white and his shivering had stopped by then. They bandaged him quickly and called for help from the deckhands to lift him up onto the gurney. It took four of them, but they finally got him into the ambulance and off to the hospital. To the deckhands and others at the scene, it looked like he was already dead.

Later that night, the wharfinger on duty—the same one who had given me the ultimatum—locked up the Rhonda with one of the padlocks they kept in the office. The next day, a work party cleared the garbage off the decks and washed them down. Someone had to pay for the work, the head wharfinger said, looking at me pointedly, and the moorage hadn't been paid. Somewhat more pointedly, I asked her if she knew whether Lyall had actually died, or if he was still alive. She flushed at this, and replied that she heard that he had survived but understood he was still in hospital. I left without offering to pay for the work or the moorage.

Lyall was in St. Paul's Hospital, located across the Burrard Street Bridge and a few blocks from the harbour. It was the same hospital where Lou had been sent to die. I hated hospitals, but feeling I had a part in Lyall's misfortune, I went to visit him that same afternoon. He was in a ward with three old men. Lying on his stomach with the back of his gown open, his feet splayed out, and only his middle covered by a sheet, he looked like a giant sleeping cherub, a hairy one. Two of the other old men in the ward were asleep too, on their backs with heads thrown back, mouths open, snoring. The third old man was sitting up in bed gumming away at an arrowroot cookie, holding it in both hands like a young child. He ignored me as I came in. I looked at the bare-knuckle brawling champeen of Britannia Beach lying there, and couldn't think of a fate any worse for someone like him.

A nurse came in at that point, saving me from the growing thought of how this was partly my fault. She was crisp and earnest, a recent graduate from a nursing school from the look of her. Her badge identified her as a registered nurse, and a nametag as Catherine.

"Friend of yours?" she asked brightly.

"More like the bane of my existence."

"Yours too, huh?" she laughed.

"He's like that in here too, is he?"

"Oh yes! We've got to keep him knocked out so he doesn't hurt somebody. Took a swing at a doctor the other day."

"Sounds like my man all right. How long are you keeping him?"

"Oh, not too long, we hope. He's had a deep tear into his gluteus maximum with some sort of filthy hook."

"A pike pole, I heard. It was filthy all right."

"Oh, you were there then?" she asked.

"No, but I know his boat and the condition it was in. The pike pole was off that boat."

"Oh. Anyway, one side of his rump is a mass of stitches. He's had a serious infection and he's still on antibiotics by an IV feed, as you can see."

"That's rough. And you'll keep him knocked out for the whole time?"

"We'll see what the doctor wants to do. We're keeping him sedated for the time being," she said.

"Well, thanks; I guess there's no point in hanging around. Those flowers on the table aren't for him, are they?"

"In fact, they are. Why do you ask?"

"They're not from someone named Judy, are they?"

"I don't think so. The lady that brought them in said her name was Rose. In fact, she comes every day just about now." From the way she said it, I gathered Rose hadn't made herself welcome.

The nurse looked at her patients in turn and bustled out. I was just about to follow her when a woman came into the ward. She was the kind of woman who didn't so much enter a room as invade it. There was a scowl on her face and her lower lip was thrust out as if she had a wad of Copenhagen between it and her teeth and was getting ready to spit. Her eyes swept over everything in the room, including me, as she went over to Lyall's bed. Putting her hand on his shoulder, she bent over and said something to him I couldn't hear. She was wearing a denim jacket over a grey sweatshirt, faded jeans, and Kodiak boots that squeaked on the waxed tile floor. When he didn't respond she straightened up and looked right at me. It felt like a push. She looked to be in her forties, big, and not the fragile type. With makeup, she could have been striking, especially the way her brows and cheekbones set off her eyes. I noticed that she had pulled in her lower lip and stopped scowling, and that her eyes were tawny, like Stalin's.

"You here visiting Lyall?" she asked in a voice that was huskier than that of some men I knew.

"Yeah. I just heard about what happened."

"You don't look like any of his friends." She looked me over like I was a horse for sale, and I couldn't say whether she approved or not.

"Say, wait a minute; you're the guy who sold him that boat!"

"Yep, that was me all right." I expected her to blame me for Lyall's troubles. Instead she threw back her head and laughed.

"Oh man, you're the guy got rooked for a grand on the deal? You must be the only guy Lyall rooked in his whole life."

"I take it you haven't seen the boat," I said.

"Not yet, I haven't. Why? What's wrong with it?"

"Nothing's wrong with it. It's just a bit run-down, but basically a good boat."

"Uh huh. Well, I'll go see for myself, now that you mention it. You better not have screwed him on that deal, mister."

"I didn't, don't worry. Anyhow, I've got to get going. If you're around, tell him I said hello. I might drop in again later. Tell him I'd like to hear the ending of that story about Judy."

She laughed again. "So he's been telling you that Judy story, has he? Yeah, I'll tell him when he wakes up."

I started to leave, but then remembered that one of my reasons for visiting was to remind Lyall that the wharfinger still wanted a copy of the blue book proving the Rhonda was his.

"By the way, did Lyall tell you about getting a copy of his boat's Ships Registry Blue Book to the wharfinger?"

"The what? No, he didn't."

"Well, here's the deal we made." I went on to explain why I had listed the Rhonda with the Ships Registry. When I got into the part about transferring the salmon licence and how I was trying to protect my interests, she smiled.

"So you wanna get a bigger boat outta this smaller licence on Lyall's boat, an' this is how it's done? What a shyster!" She kept smiling when she said this.

"It's all perfectly legal," I said.

"Sounds like it." Her smile had turned into a grin, taking twenty years off her face.

"You don't sound like you believe me."

"Believe you! Lookit, our old man spent his life hand-loggin up by Lund. Them bastards from fisheries harassed him for years about messin up the streams, just because he was a little guy. The big outfits right next door that really messed up everything, they didn't bother. If you're screwin them somehow, good on ya."

"You said 'our old man,' so Lyall's your brother?"

"Yep, my dimwit big brother." She said it in a way that changed my entire first impression of her charging into the ward.

"And your son works at the Hotel Vancouver?"

"What?" Her eyes narrowed. "Oh, I get it, Lyall's fancy woman from back east again."

"None of my business, but Lyall started telling me about her and never got to tell me how it turned out."

"Yeah, well, don't ask me. Jake, that's my boy, told me somethin about it. Lyall's had such a string of women hangin on him over the years, I never paid much attention to any of it."

"Really?"

"Yep, believe it or not. Takes after the old man that way. The old bugger's still like that and he's pushing eighty in an old folks' home."

We talked a while longer in the ward and then in the cafeteria where we had a coffee afterwards. Rose was like one of those passengers you sit beside on a Greyhound bus;

they start talking and tell intimate details about their family history to complete strangers. She told me about her oldest brother, a logger like the old man, who died in a falling accident, and how Lyall got into a fight with the old man because of it, then left home shortly afterwards. A year later she left home too, and got pregnant at seventeen by a guy in the city who was twice her age and had a nice car. Going back home with her baby didn't work out; neither did a quick marriage to a guy she knew from high school.

She left her son with her mother for a while and went to California, hoping to ride her looks into the movies. When she saw that her chances of getting auditions depended on agents getting into her pants, she gave up on the idea. At a party in San Francisco she met a biker named Sonny Barger and became his woman until she refused to get a "Property of the Hell's Angels" tattoo on her butt. Still in California, where they had such things, she wrestled in a ladies' circuit for a while but was kicked out for being too rough. She found work in bars, and I had an impression she might have turned a trick or two just to get by. After a couple of years, she headed north and reclaimed her boy.

Back in Vancouver, she got a job driving a coffee truck to construction sites and the waterfront, where longshoremen were unloading ships. The work suited her, and she eventually bought her own truck, which she still drove. Her boy grew up and went out on his own. A few years later, while shopping at Woodward's, she ran into a longshoreman who used to buy coffee from her truck. He had been retired for a few years. His wife had died and he was lonely. One thing led to another, and in a few months she had moved into his house. I asked if she was happy with him, and she asked what I meant by "happy." We talked for a couple of hours, or more correctly, she talked and I mostly listened. As we were leaving, she gave me a bear hug and a kiss on the cheek and said it was too bad I hadn't been around twenty years ago.

I went back to spending all my time working on the new boat, and didn't hear any more about Lyall until weeks later. Pete, who had been keeping an eye on the *Ruby Dawn*, phoned one evening to tell me some guy from up north had been looking her over a couple of days running. He looked interested and sounded like he had money; I should expect a call soon, he thought. It was late and he knew I had to be up early, but before he hung up, Pete asked if I'd heard about Lyall.

I hadn't, so Pete gave me the short version. Lyall was discharged from hospital a week or so after my visit and moved back aboard his boat. By then his neighbours were badgering the wharfinger's office about a gasoline smell, arguing the *Rhonda* should be towed away because of the danger to other boats. When nothing was done, someone began cutting Lyall's mooring lines at night. The *Rhonda* would drift away on the tide and he would wake up in a surprise new location the next morning. Finding his way back, he'd raise hell with his neighbours, trying to find out who'd cut the lines. But he was just a shell of his old self, and all he got back were taunts and laughter. This went on for a few weeks until one night someone cut his lines yet again, and in the morning the *Rhonda* didn't come back.

Nobody knew or cared where Lyall had gone, but Pete, decent man that he was, felt badly about his part in moving him and kept asking around. He had just heard that the *Rhonda* was tied up at the government dock in Lund with a new paint job. From what Rose had told me about their early life, it sounded like Lyall had gone back to his roots. I left it at that. The loose end, as Valerie called it, had been tied up.

I never did find out how the story about Judy and Lyall ended, or if it had even happened at all. After that day at the hospital listening to Rose's stories, I couldn't help but wonder if telling wild tales wasn't a family trait. But maybe

Lyall's story about Judy was too outrageous not to be true. Some stories are like that.

Somehow clearing up that loose end was the shot of energy I needed to focus totally on building the new boat. Until then, it didn't look like I could meet the schedule I had drawn up. After that, I didn't have any doubts at all. As if on cue, the *Ruby Dawn* sold, ensuring we'd have the money needed to finish what we'd started.

Building the boat that winter became one of the most satisfying times in my life. Ideas on doing complicated things with wood came welling up from what must have been passed on to me by my father. I taught myself the systems needed, like hydraulics, AC and DC electric power, diesel fuel filtration, and hot and cold pressurized water, and put all of them in myself. The engine, a Detroit Diesel 6V53, I put in without help, too. Even what I'd learned in architectural school came into play in designing a good-looking boat from the engine room to the main cabin and especially the forward sleeping quarters. Valerie came aboard often, with growing excitement about how much easier fishing was going to be after two boats without a proper head. In a few more months we launched a boat far beyond anything I could have imagined while taking those first swipes at re-caulking the poor old *T.K.*

The best part was the sense of accomplishment that drives life forward. It didn't come from studying architecture. It started from merely watching a gillnet's drift.

||| GILLNETTING TERMS AND DEFINITIONS |||

Beam sea Wind and waves perpendicular to a boat's side, often causing the vessel to roll violently.

Book (fish) Record of a gillnetter's catch by weight and species. This was the basis for paying the gillnetter for the year's catch. Supplies bought at the fishing company's store, net-mending services, etc. would be deducted from these earnings.

Boundary Perimeter indicated by triangular markers. Fishing was not permitted inside the boundary to protect spawning salmon at the mouths of rivers, creeks, and some bays.

Bull-nosing Rounding off corners of trim used along edges of wooden boats, that is, along wheelhouse and cabin tops.

Checker Small fish hold, usually alongside the drum.

Chrysler Crown Six-cylinder marine engine made by Chrysler, often found in older gillnetters.

Clove hitch A fast way to tie up a boat, usually to the edge timber found on most docks.

Cockpit Space at the stern of a fishboat where catch is retrieved; the term usually applies to trollers but is also used by gillnetters.

Collector Boat used by the fishing companies to collect, weigh, and book fish from gillnetters on their sets, usually every morning.

Company flag Small flag in a company's design and colour, flown from the mast of gillnetters to identify them to company collectors making the rounds to collect fish.

Cork (someone) Set a gillnet parallel to another gillnetter's set closer than one net's length away so as to obstruct the other's fishing ability.

Cork line A line strung with corks about five inches long and three inches in diameter that support the top of a gillnet when set.

Dark set A set made just before dusk and picked after dark.

Dawn set A set made just before dawn and picked after daylight.

Dock see **Float**.

Doghouse Small wheelhouse with only enough room for the skipper.

Double-ender Vessel with a canoe stern.

Drogue A canvas bag, or anything suitable, on a line thrown overboard to provide drag to keep a boat's bow (or stern) into the wind.

Drum Spool-shaped reel for holding the net aboard a gillnetter.

Drum drive Transmission providing power to turn the drum. Many were adapted from Ford rear-ends, but the best were purpose-made by Easthope. Current drives are usually hydraulic.

Easthope British Columbia manufacturer of one- or two-cylinder gasoline engines often found on early-twentieth-century gillnetters, and later, drum drives.

False Creek Fishermen's Terminal Fishboat harbour in downtown Vancouver.

Finger float Small, narrow dock at right angles to a main dock that ran along the entire length of a boat tied up to it.

Fire in the water Phosphorescent marine organisms that cling to the net at night, making it highly visible to fish.

Fish camp Facility owned by a fishing company that includes fuel tanks, net loft, mending racks, tool crib, ice plant, laundry, and general store, all usually mounted on a scow to which mooring docks for fishboats are attached. The scows were usually towed into place before the start of fishing season. Larger camps would have hundreds of boats moored between openings.

Fishing companies The businesses that bought fish from fishermen. The largest ones were BC Packers and the Canadian Fishing Company. A smaller one was named Francis Millerd and Company.

Fishing lights Lights on the mast and sometimes the boom when a vessel is lying on a set at night.

Float Dock, usually of timber, constructed on flotation material to which boats are moored.

Gillnetter Boat or person fishing by means of a net two hundred fathoms long (twelve hundred feet) and sixty meshes deep (depending on mesh size and hangings, about thirty feet deep).

Gurdies Brass spools, usually in sets of three, four, or sometimes five used for holding trolling wire, installed on each side of the cockpit.

Head Toilet (newer boats often had a hand basin and shower in the head).

High boat Boat delivering the largest catch.

Highliner Top producer.

Hull speed The speed at which a hull travels most efficiently for the energy used to propel it.

Iron mike Autopilot.

Jog Detach the boat from the net (usually when a boat pulls the net out of its proper set) and idle near the net's end. Jogging usually occurs with heavier, newer boats that aren't double-enders.

Lazarette Space under boat stern housing rudder stock and sometimes fuel tanks.

Lump Wave; as in "it's getting lumpy" when the sea turns rough.

Mickey Mouse CB radio.

Narrow-gutted A boat with a relatively small beam compared to its length.

Net in the wheel A gillnet caught in the boat's propeller.

On the dry Out of the water for storage or hull work.

Packer Larger vessel that receives fish collected from gill-netters and runs its load to Vancouver for processing and distribution.

Pick (the net) Remove fish (and anything else) from the net.

Rolling chocks Longitudinal wooden fins bolted to hulls not equipped with stabilizers to lessen vessels' tendency to roll.

Romeos A type of boot without laces, favoured by some fishermen for the ease with which they could be put on or taken off. Blundstones are modelled after them.

Run the net Detach the boat from the net and run along its length to check the set for fish or problems. At night, a spotlight or docking lights are used.

Scotchman An inflatable red buoy used to mark the end of a gillnet set during daylight hours.

Screaming Jimmy Two-stroke diesel engine made by Detroit Diesel, so called because of noise created.

Seiner Large boat that fishes with a net that closes to form a purse, which does not allow catch to escape. Seiners are used for salmon and herring.

Scow Flat-bottomed boat used as a barge.

Set Put a gillnet into position for fishing; also a gillnet that has been so deployed.

Side locker See **Checker**.

Smiley Spring (Chinook) salmon larger than thirty pounds, named because of the smile on any fisherman who catches one.

Stabilizer poles Poles mounted mid-ship on each side rail of the vessel, supported against mast crosstree when not in use. When deployed, the poles lean out at approximately a 45-degree angle to keep stabilizers clear of hull.

Stabilizers Small finned weights suspended about six feet into the water from stabilizer poles, used to steady vessels in heavy seas.

Stern rollers Roller assembly made up of horizontal and vertical rollers used for guiding gillnets being set or being reeled in.

Tide rip A stretch of rough water caused by the meeting of currents.

Think like a baby Term for mental lapses due to long periods without sleep, first heard from Croatian fishermen.

Trunk cabin Compartment forward of and lower than the wheelhouse, containing bunks and galley.

Ways A marine railway used for hauling boats out of the water to allow them to be worked on.

Weed line A light line attached along the top of the net that is hung from the cork line by twine. It allows for about ten inches between the cork line and the weed line when the net is deployed. The weed line is used in waters where floating seaweed is common to let the seaweed float under the cork line and over the net without being caught.

Wheel Propeller.

⫿ ABOUT THE AUTHOR ⫿

William Nicholas Marach was born and raised in Wawa, a Northern Ontario mining town. Nick studied architecture at the University of Manitoba, but left during his fourth year and hitchhiked across the prairies in mid-winter. He somehow reached Vancouver alive, then worked at several jobs before resuming his studies at UBC the following year. He received a Bachelor of Architecture in 1968.

After graduating, Nick worked in an architectural firm in Toronto then travelled extensively by motorcycle in England, Europe, and North Africa before returning to Vancouver in 1972. He fished out of Vancouver from 1972 until 1982, while working as at architect at several different firms.

In 1982, Nick moved with his family to Yellowknife, NWT. He was appointed Chief Architect of the NWT in 1984 and then Assistant Deputy Minister of Public Works before leaving the North in 1992. He continued to fish during long summer vacations spent in Vancouver and by flying to Vancouver for salmon openings in the fall.

He sold his last gillnet boat in 1990 and bought a fifty-foot Monk McQueen cruiser, the Fort Rupert, which he extensively rebuilt, then sold in 2000. He intends to spend the next ten years of his life writing and the ten beyond that painting.